What readers are saying about
TextMate: Power Editing for the Mac

This is not just a book, but a doorway to higher dimensional text editing! By the third chapter I was completely switched over to TextMate from Vim. The book provided everything I needed to take full advantage of all that TextMate offers. This book rocks, and James is my new hero.

► **Ernest Obusek**
   Software Engineer, Network Appliance, Inc.

This book is outstanding. Without saying it, James has made the case for TextMate quickly becoming *the* interface for 90% of what any OS X user will ever need to do. I've read a substantial amount of material concerning both OS X and TextMate, but by Chapter 3, James had blown me away. By the end of Chapter 5 . . . wow. This is some powerful stuff.

► **Stephen Hargrove**
   System Administrator

As an Emacs junkie, it takes considerable persuasion for me to even consider using another editor. This book did the job, and now I use TextMate regularly. The chapters on the various built-in automations, scripting and snippets are invaluable. Ruby on Rails and other coding enthusiasts will also find that this book provides ample coverage of programming oriented tasks.

► **Jon Mountjoy**
   Director, MemeStorm Ltd.

I've been using TextMate for months and I thought I knew everything it could do. I was surprised to discover many editing tricks and key-commands that I had completely missed. James did a terrific job making this book an essential asset for even a seasoned TextMate user.

► **Michael Gregoire**
   Owner/Creator, nvzion.com and blocSonic.com

TextMate is like an onion. It seems like such a simple thing when you first see it, then you start peeling back layers and suddenly discover the richness that lies underneath. This book peels the onion that is TextMate, revealing the awesome power underneath. It has become my Swiss-army chainsaw, flexible enough for everything and powerful enough for anything.

▶ **Neal Ford**
Application Architect, ThoughtWorks

A thorough, practical reference for anyone who ever wondered if there was more to life than Dreamweaver.

▶ **Benjamin Jackson**
Technical Director, INCOMUM Design and Concept

This beautifully written text brings the power of TextMate to someone who does not know any programming language. Each page reveals hidden, indispensable tricks that improve work flow, which is what the TextMate philosophy is all about.

▶ **Jenny Harrison**
Professor of Mathematics, UC Berkeley

TextMate

Power Editing for the Mac

TextMate
Power Editing for the Mac

James Edward Gray II

The Pragmatic Bookshelf
Raleigh, North Carolina   Dallas, Texas

Our Pragmatic courses, workshops, and other products can help you and your team create better software and have more fun. For more information, as well as the latest Pragmatic titles, please visit us at

http://www.pragmaticprogrammer.com

ISBN-10: 0-9787392-3-X

ISBN-13: 978-0-9787392-3-2

Printed on acid-free paper with 85% recycled, 30% post-consumer content.

First printing, January, 2007

Version: 2007-1-29

*"James enjoys playing chess
and loves his mother very much."*

*For Nicole and Payden, a sister and brother so cool
they make me look good, and the Payne women
who remain my biggest fans.*

Contents

Chapter 1

Introduction

You probably spend most of your day reading and writing text in one form or another. Programmers write text in arcane languages with unusual rules. Web developers produce HTML and CSS files by the pound, and those are just another flavor of plain old text. Even Ph.D. candidates tend to generate massive amounts of text that can be typeset using LaTeX or similar tools.

Now think about it: If you take the time to learn enough to trim even a few steps off your daily workflow, that's going to add up to be a big win in very little time. The great news is that you can probably save a lot of work with just a little knowledge. This book is full of timesaving techniques that pay off immediately.

So, which text editor should you learn? This is a heated topic in computer geek circles. Those on each side of the famous vi versus emacs debate are religious about their choice. You can use what you want, but I've worked with a few editors now, and TextMate is the right fit for me. In this short book, I'll show you how to automate much of your daily workflow and try to make a true TextMate believer out of you too.

1.1 A Brief History of TextMate

TextMate was created by Allan Odgaard in 2004 while he was waiting to start a new job. After a couple of months of work, he announced the first release of the editor. It was a little slim.

There were no preferences to set, and you couldn't print with it. Less than two years later, TextMate was awarded the Apple Design Award for Best Developer Tool. As I write this introduction, TextMate has registered users in the tens of thousands. People have certainly started to take note of the little editor. It even has preferences and can print these days. Allan never quite made it to that other job, but instead spends his time improving TextMate for us users.

What has made TextMate so successful in such a short time is that it combines the power of Unix with the accessibility of Mac OS X. The many Unix tools are a powerful addition to the user's tool belt. Unix editors such as vi and emacs have been enormously successful because they tie in so well to these tools. For Mac users, though, these editors have painfully foreign interfaces.

TextMate really makes a great effort to expose these helpers to the user from a Mac-friendly interface. The automations really shine for this. You can wrap a few operations useful for a common task together and package them in a single menu item or keystroke. This helps users create tailored enhancements to TextMate for each domain with which they need to work.

Even better, TextMate makes it easy to share these specialized automations with others. That has given birth to a vibrant open source–like community sharing their TextMate enhancements, though the application itself remains proprietary. Today the official TextMate Subversion repository holds more than 125 groupings of automations and languages maintained by dozens of developers.

You can even download tools to work with spreadsheet data[1] or screenplays[2] in the editor. Odds are good TextMate already covers at least some of your needs, and for the situations where it doesn't, you can train it yourself.

That's what this book is all about. I'll show you how to use the built-in automations and teach you how to take your editing to the next level by building your own. You'll get the raw power of Unix, filtered for Mac user consumption.

---

1. http://skiadas.dcostanet.net/afterthought/2006/04/20/more-spreadsheets-in-textmate/
2. http://ollieman.net/code/screenwriting/textmate/

1.2 In These Pages

Going forward, I will cover a subset of TextMate capabilities that can turn anyone into a power user. Different users need to learn different features, though, so I've tried to lay out the information so you can conveniently get to what you need. This book details editing tips, automations, and TextMate's knowledge of languages:

Editing

In this part of the book, I will cover basic text editing with TextMate. Chapters include information for working with TextMate projects, editing text with an emphasis on moving around and making selections, and using *regular expressions* for super find-and-replace operations.

Though these are the basics, they build a foundation for working with TextMate's automations, and I'll sneak in enough tricks to help you impress your geek friends.

Automations

Here we will delve into the heart of TextMate. I'll show you how to use the most popular automations included with the application. You will get a lot of mileage out of these tools, I promise.

From there, this part turns to building your own automations so you can customize how TextMate helps you work. I'll show you how to build *snippets* to insert bits of customizable content into any document, how to record and replay your way past repetitive changes with *macros*, and how to introduce intelligent behaviors into TextMate with *commands*. This part closes with some tips from the automation pros.

Languages, preferences, and themes

The last leg of our journey provides detailed coverage of how to teach TextMate to read new languages and how to build themes to support them. I will also cover how to tweak TextMate's smart editing features.

This is your chance to fit your pet dialects into the TextMate mold, allowing you to build custom automations targeted specifically at the needs of the language.

Along the way you will also find the following:

Menu References

When describing TextMate's features I will often need to refer to commands selected from the menus. I will use a common shorthand for this, so when you see Edit → Find → Find, that means that you should select Find from the Find submenu in the Edit menu. My hope is that the shorthand is actually more natural, since it displays the items in the order you need to select them.

Live code

Most of the examples used in this book come from a bundle of automations I built while writing the book. You can download[3] this bundle and play with the examples inside TextMate. If you see a marker line like the one that follows at the top of a listing in the book, that means you can find the code in the download:

language_grammars/json.textmate

```
constant = {
  name = 'constant.language.json';
  match = '\b(?:true|false|null)\b';
};
```

If you're reading the PDF version of this book and if your PDF viewer supports hyperlinks, you can click the marker, and the code should appear in a browser window. Some browsers (such as Safari) might mistakenly try to interpret some of the code as HTML. If this happens, view the source of the page to see the real source code.

Joe Asks...

Joe, the mythical developer, sometimes pops up to ask questions about stuff I talk about in the text. I answer these questions as I go along.

Before you jump right into playing with the editor, I need to cover one last convention used in this book.

1.3 The Mac Keyboard and Mouse

To really learn TextMate, you must break down and learn a set of keyboard shortcuts. It will change the way you work, I promise. TextMate

---

3. From http://www.pragmaticprogrammer.com/titles/textmate/code.html

will show you the keystrokes in several parts of the interface. Here's
your cheat sheet:[4]

^ The Control or Ctrl key.

⌥ The Option or Alt key.

⇧ The Shift key.

⌘ The Command key. This always has an Apple logo on the key.

⇥ The Tab key.

⇤ Not an actual key. This back-tab is produced when pressing Tab
   while holding the Shift key.

↩ The Return key.

⌤ The Enter key—Fn plus Return on a laptop without a dedicated
   key.

⌫ The Delete or Backspace key.

⌦ The Del key—Fn plus Delete on my laptop keyboard. This is often
   referred to as *forward delete*.

⎋ The Escape or Esc key.

← The left arrow key.

→ The right arrow key.

↑ The up arrow key.

↓ The down arrow key.

⇞ The Page Up key—Fn plus the up arrow on my laptop keyboard.

⇟ The Page Down key—Fn plus the down arrow on my laptop keyboard.

↖ The Home key—Fn plus the left arrow on my laptop keyboard.

↘ The End key—Fn plus the right arrow on my laptop keyboard.

⑦ The Help key. This key is not available on laptop keyboards.

You should know three other facts about Mac keyboard shortcuts as
they are displayed both in TextMate and in this book. First, keyboard
shortcuts with letters are always shown with the capital letter for easier
identification, but you only need to add a ⇧ to the keystroke if the
symbol is actually displayed in the keyboard shortcut. For example,
^ R doesn't require a ⇧ even though the R shown is capitalized, but
^ ⇧ R would because you see the symbol.

Along similar lines, symbol-based keystrokes such as ^ < may not display a needed ⇧. On some keyboards, that action involves two keys,
but on my U.S. key layout I need a ⇧ to type a < character. Thus, for
me the keystroke is actually ^ ⇧ <.

---

4. If you would like to be able to type these glyphs yourself, refer to the documentation
at http://macromates.com/blog/archives/2006/07/10/multi-stroke-key-bindings/.

A third tip to make note of is that laptop users trying to use keyboard shortcuts involving the function keys may actually adjust their screen brightness instead. When this happens, you can add the Fn key to the keystroke to get it to activate. However, the operating system seems to have a glitch regarding these keystrokes that sometimes requires you to press the Fn key after any other modifier keys. So if the TextMate keystroke is ⌘ F2, you might need to press ⌘, then Fn, and then F2. If you get tired of this finger dance and don't mind relegating brightness adjustment to the Fn-enhanced keystroke, there is a checkbox for this in the Keyboard tab of the Keyboard & Mouse panel of System Preferences, available from the Apple menu.

I will also cover how to use the mouse with TextMate. Most Apple machines still ship with a one-button mouse. You could always right-click on Mac OS X with a one-button mouse by holding down the ⌃ key and clicking. In this book, two-button-mouse users should translate a click into left-click and ⌃-click into right-click.

1.4 Installing TextMate and Tools

If you don't already have TextMate installed, drop by the TextMate website http://macromates.com/, click the Download link in the top-right position of the sidebar, and drag the application out of the archive you downloaded and onto your Mac's Applications directory. Installing Text-Mate is really that easy, but keep reading for details on a few more helpers you can add.

When you first launch a recent version of TextMate, it should open an Enhanced Terminal Usage dialog box, offering to install the *mate* command-line tool. If you missed that dialog box, you can always get back to it by choosing Help → Terminal Usage. Either way, I highly recommend doing the install. The mate tool is described in the sidebar on the facing page; I'll show you more tricks with it as we move along.

You don't want to miss one other install. If you haven't already, select Bundles → TextMate → Install "Edit in TextMate". This installs an input manager, which will allow you to edit the content of other applications, such as Mail and Safari,[5] using TextMate. Try it: Open Safari, browse to http://google.com/, place your caret in the search box, trigger Edit → Edit in TextMate (⌃ ⌘ E), type a search topic, and save (⌘ S) and close (⌘ W)

---

5. This works only for Cocoa applications.

Command-Line TextMate

Though TextMate is a modern Mac application with a nice user interface, it can interact flawlessly with Unix tools accessed from the Terminal. The bridge is the mate command-line tool.

Adding mate to commands will cause TextMate to activate and allow you to create or edit some content, which can be further processed by other commands. To edit a file in TextMate, just invoke mate file_name_here. You can also pipe content into a TextMate window for you to work with. For example, this command shows a directory listing in TextMate: ls | mate.

Another great feature of mate is its ability to wait on you to edit and return the content to the calling process. This allows you to use it as a standard Unix editor by adding the -w flag. For example, my bash .profile file (loaded each time I start a new session in the Terminal) contains the following lines that allow me to use TextMate as my editor for version control commit messages, and much more:

```
export EDITOR="mate -w"
export CVSEDITOR="mate -w"
export SVN_EDITOR="mate -w"
```

There's more to the mate command, so be sure to read the built-in Help by typing mate -h in the Terminal.

the TextMate document to push the content back to Safari. TextMate isn't a lot of help for content this size, but imagine editing wiki pages or long emails. It's worth the effort to memorize that keyboard shortcut for these occasions.

A final step I recommend taking to set up TextMate is to "live on the edge." Many pieces of software offer "edge" releases nowadays for those who like being the first to explore new features. Often these releases are only lightly tested and still pretty fragile. TextMate is evolving fast now, though, with a decent focus on refinement. This means the cutting-edge versions usually have more bug fixes and are actually safer. I think that's worth being hassled for a few seconds every couple of days by the automatic upgrade system. If you agree, you can turn it on by selecting TextMate → Preferences (⌘ ,), clicking the Software Update icon, and changing the Watch For menu to Cutting-Edge.

If You Already Had TextMate Installed

It is possible to download extras for TextMate, and it's common for people to do this. Unfortunately, this sometimes hides some built-in enhancements if you forget to keep the add-ons up-to-date. Therefore, I recommend you do not install any extras you don't need.

This book deals only with items included in a regular TextMate install, and I don't begin to cover all of it. TextMate itself has a lot of functionality, so be sure it in fact doesn't meet your needs before you decide to add on to it.

If you have downloaded any extras and you have trouble with the steps in this book, I recommend returning to a default TextMate install.[6] If you still cannot find some item I refer to in the Bundles menu, you probably have it disabled. You can check what TextMate is currently loading by choosing Bundles → Bundle Editor → Show Bundle Editor (^ ⌥ ⌘ B) and clicking the Filter List button at the bottom of that dialog box. Feel free to disable any languages you don't usually work with,[7] but see Chapter 5, *Built-in Automations*, on page 53 for some details about what I find useful.

If you are in need of something missing from the default install, Get-Bundle is the safest and easiest tool to use to add on to TextMate. See http://macromates.com/blog/archives/2006/08/21/getting-more-bundles/ for more information.

1.5   The Editing Window

When you are past all the installing, you should be greeted by the editing window when you launch TextMate. You will spend plenty of time interacting with this window, so it's worth recognizing the various parts of it. Use Figure 1.1, on the facing page, as a reference.

Aside from the typical Mac window elements such as the Close, Minimize, and Maximize buttons in the title bar and the scroll bar down the right side, a TextMate window has two unique elements. First, the bar that runs down the left side of the window is known as the *gutter*. In the

---

6.   See http://macromates.com/wiki/Troubleshooting/RevertToDefaultBundles.
7.   Do mind the warning at the bottom of the dialog box about the bundles that should not be disabled, though.

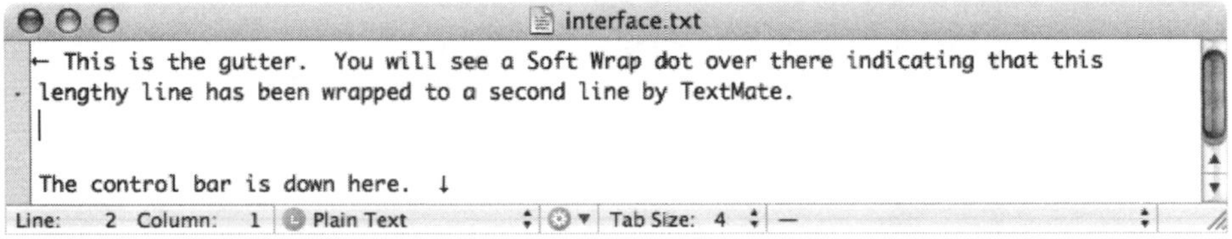

Figure 1.1: THE EDITING WINDOW

figure you can see the Soft Wrap indicator dots there. You can configure exactly what shows up in the gutter through View → Gutter.

Second, the bottom of the editing window contains a control bar with various items. The first panel gives a readout of the current caret position in the document (line and column position). Following that, you have a set of four pop-up menus.

The first is the language menu that you can use to set the language for the current document. This influences TextMate's syntax highlighting, among other features. The second menu is the automation menu, which is just a shortcut for reaching most of the items in the Bundles menu. Users tend to access this menu via ^ ◌, use the arrow keys to navigate, and press ↵ to make a selection. The third menu is for controlling TextMate's tab behaviors described in Section 3.3, *Working with Tabs*, on page 35, and the fourth is the symbol menu described in Section 3.1, *Moving to a Line, Symbol, or Bookmark*, on page 23.

Now that you know what these elements are called, it's time to find out what you can accomplish with them!

Part I

Editing

Chapter 2

Projects

I'm assuming you are familiar with text editors. You know how to create a new file and open existing files. You know how to cut and paste and print your document. Most of this book will be devoted to showing you the power that TextMate gives you for authoring and editing files, but in this chapter I thought I'd start with something most editors don't do: working with *projects*.

TextMate allows you to create a project of related files and work with them as a group. Since most nontrivial projects will involve manipulating several files, this can be a real boon to helping you manage them.

2.1 Creating a Project

It's not hard to get started with TextMate's projects. You can just create a blank project and add to it as needed. Select File → New Project (^ ⌘ N). The blank project window will include a big hint for the next step, and, as it says, you can just drag files and folders into the project drawer. Try this with any files you have handy. As you drop them in the drawer, they will become part of a file listing displayed in the drawer.

You are free to arrange the list of files in the project drawer by dragging them into the desired order with the mouse. You can also create groups for the files using the folder button at the bottom of the project drawer or by ⌘-clicking several files and selecting Group Selected Files from the action menu at the bottom of the project drawer, as shown in Figure 2.1, on the next page. The file order and groups are strictly for your reference.

Figure 2.1: Grouping project files

You can control the side of the window on which the project drawer is displayed. It defaults to appearing on the left, but you can move it with these steps:

1. Select View → Hide Project Drawer (^ ⌥ ⌘ D), if the drawer is currently visible.
2. Move the project window close enough to the edge of the screen so the drawer doesn't have room to open on the side you don't want it on.
3. Bring the drawer back with View → Show Project Drawer (^ ⌥ ⌘ D).

TextMate will remember your drawer side preference, as long as new windows have room to open it on the favored side.

When you have the project the way you want it, choose File → Save Project (^ ⌘ S). This action causes TextMate to save a file of project details. You will be able to reload this file at any time in the future to have TextMate restore the files of the project, which files you had open, and project-specific settings. Furthermore, TextMate will remember if you quit with a saved project open and will reopen it for you to resume working with when you relaunch TextMate.

2.2 Moving between Files

The main point of placing files in a project is to quickly have access to those files. You can use the mouse to open as many files as you need to open. A single-click opens the file in TextMate, as long as TextMate believes the file is a text file. It will look for known text extensions or scan the first 8KB of a file to see whether it is valid UTF-8 text (a super-set of ASCII) to determine this.

If you need to correct TextMate's guess about a file, just highlight it in the project drawer, and choose Treat Files with "ext" Extension as Binary/Text from the action menu at the bottom of the project drawer. TextMate will remember this setting for the file type in the future. Double-clicking a file will open it in the default application for files of that type, which may not be TextMate.

You can navigate the project drawer completely by using your keyboard as well. Use ^ →| to toggle the keyboard focus between the editing window and the project drawer. When the drawer has the focus, use ↑ and ↓ to move the selection up and down the drawer. You can press → to expand folder or group listings and ← to collapse them. When you have reached the file you want to open, a simple ↵ is equivalent to a single-click of the mouse. You can also tap the spacebar with a selection in the project drawer to expose an in-place editor for renaming the file.

The previously described system for opening files is fine when you are browsing. When you know where you want to go, you can use a faster and better way, which I'll teach you now.

When you want to move to a file you know the name of, start by opening the Navigation → Go to File dialog box. Definitely spend the effort to learn the keyboard shortcut for this one; it is ⌘T for "To." This dialog box lists every file in your project sorted with the most recently used files at the top of the list. This makes it a fast means to switch back and forth between a few files. You can use the ↑ and ↓ arrows to move the selection and ↵ to dismiss the dialog box and open the selected file.

What makes this dialog box even more powerful, though, is the ability to type an abbreviation that TextMate can use to filter the file list. The letters you type do not need to be together in the filename, so you can generally just use the first letter of each word. For example, to match pitches_controller_test.rb, I would use pct, as I do in Figure 2.2, on the following page. TextMate will even remember which abbreviations you

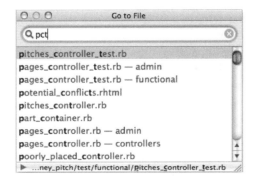

Figure 2.2: FILENAME MATCHING

use to select files in the project, adapting to your work needs when you adjust a match with the arrow keys.

Project files open in *tabs* of the project window. You can switch between tabs at any time using ⌘1 to move to the leftmost tab, using ⌘2 to move to the tab to the right of that, and using all the way up to ⌘9 to move to the ninth tab from the left. Alternately, you can use ⌥⌘← to move to the tab left of the currently active tab or ⌥⌘→ to move right. You can even use the mouse to drag tabs into the desired order to make this access more convenient, as shown in Figure 2.3, on the next page.

If you are working with a language that has header files, such as C, you will want to learn one more file navigation shortcut. You can use ⌥⌘↑ to cycle between all files with an identical base name (not counting an extension) as the file open in the current tab. A new tab will be created to hold the switched-to file, if it wasn't already open. For example, if a project contains widget.h and widget.c, you could move between these two files with just this keystroke.

2.3 Shortcuts for Creating Projects

Dragging files and folders onto TextMate by hand is just one way to create a project. An oft-used shortcut is to drag the files and folders directly onto the TextMate application icon, be it at the installed location or in your Dock. This opens or activates TextMate, creates a project, and immediately populates it with the dropped files and folders. Be warned that TextMate will not remind you to save projects created

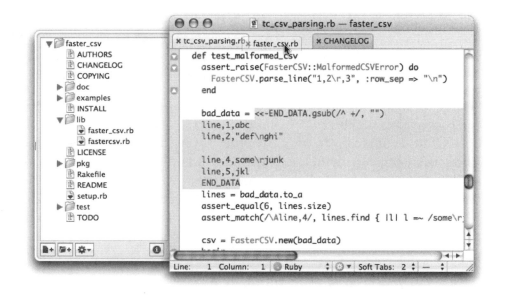

Figure 2.3: DRAGGING TABS

this way when closed, so save the project right after you open it if you want to keep it.

A third way to create projects comes in handy when working with the Terminal. If you feed the mate command multiple filenames, one or more folders, or a shell glob, it will create a project containing the indicated items. For example:

```
mate .            # a project of the current directory
mate a.txt b.txt  # a project of two files
mate *.csv        # a project of CSV files in the current directory
```

2.4 Folder References

TextMate supports two kinds of projects. You created the first type early in this chapter when you dragged in a group of files without regard to their organization on your disk. The other sort of project preserves the file system hierarchy. You get this type of project when you place folders in a project.

The folders in a project are references to the actual objects on the disk. This has two effects. First, TextMate will rescan the folders whenever the application regains focus, updating the contents in case they have changed. The second benefit is that the folder button at the bottom of the project drawer creates actual folders on the hard disk. New folders are created inside the currently selected folder in the project drawer.

With these changes, you can generally handle editing and file management operations inside TextMate and skip a few trips to the Finder. For this reason, I tend to favor TextMate projects based on folder references. Taking this one step further, I think you will find it's often beneficial to have a single top-level folder containing the whole project. The TODO command expects this setup, and it makes it easier to do project-wide commits and updates using the Subversion commands, both of which I will talk more about in Chapter 5, *Built-in Automations*, on page 53.

Projects with files and groups, on the other hand, tend to be good for times when you need to work with only a few files from various locations or when you want to rearrange the hierarchy without affecting the actual disk layout. For these reasons, such projects are often ideal for some scratch work. When I need to work with just the XML files in one directory of my project for a time or when I need to organize a bunch of files so I can see what needs changing, I build a files-and-groups project.

With either kind of project, you can use Rename or Remove Selected Files from the action menu at the bottom of the project drawer. Rename changes the actual file, and Remove Selected Files gives you the choice to move the file to the Trash or just remove the file from the project.

Both project types also support creating new files using the file button at the bottom of the project drawer. If you are using folder references, the file will be created in the selected folder. File projects will prompt you for a location to save the file.

Limiting Folder References

You also have the ability to limit files and folders included in the folder references of your project. This option is not available for the groups you create in file projects, since you can limit those by hand. To adjust the listing, select a top-level folder reference in the project drawer, and click the information button in the lower-right corner of the drawer, as shown in Figure 2.4, on the next page.

The two patterns listed here are regular expressions matched against the full file path to determine whether it should be included in the

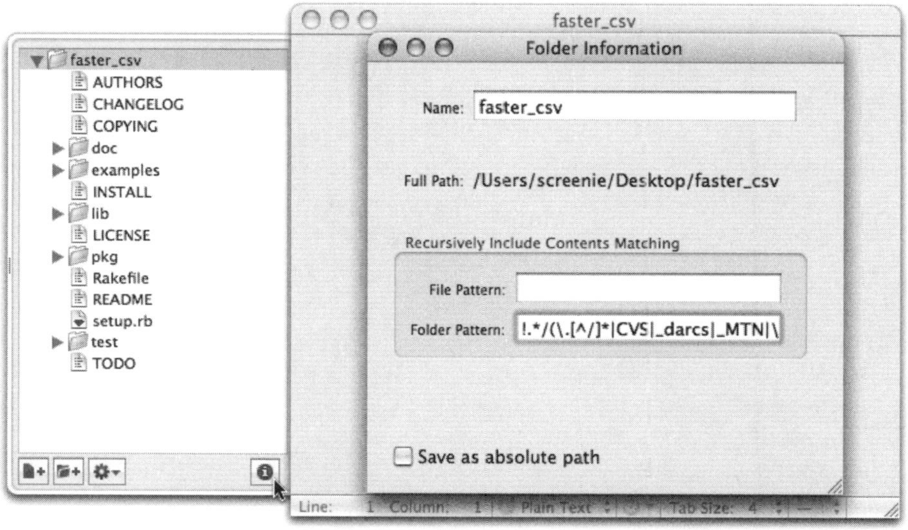

Figure 2.4: FOLDER REFERENCE PATTERNS

project listing.[1] By default, only matched files will be listed, but if the first character of the pattern is an exclamation mark, everything but the matched files will be listed. The default pattern excludes directories such as version control directories, but you may want to customize it to your needs. For example, you could exclude a vendored copy of the Ruby on Rails framework by adding |rails just before |CVS in the default pattern. You will spend a lot more time playing with regular expressions in Section 4.2, *Mixing in Regular Expressions*, on page 42.

You can modify the defaults TextMate uses for these patterns in the Advanced pane of TextMate's TextMate → Preferences dialog box (⌘ ,). Click the Folder References tab, and then modify the patterns to suit your needs. Existing projects will not be affected by changes made here.

That covers file management in TextMate. The editor makes it easy to treat the files of your project as a whole and manage them without frequent trips to the Finder. To have files, though, you need to create the content for them in the first place, and that's what the next chapter is all about.

---

1. The Save as Absolute Path checkbox on this dialog has no effect for folder references which are always stored as such.

Chapter 3

Power Editing

The main function of a text-editing program is to allow you to enter and change document content. I will talk a lot more about how TextMate can help you enter content when we get to automations, but this chapter is all about manipulating text.

TextMate provides a great deal of support for moving around your document content, selecting text, and making intelligent changes. Becoming familiar with these functions can save you so much time for tasks you will face daily.

3.1 Moving Around

When you're not typing, odds are good that you're trying to get the caret to the right place to do some more typing. TextMate provides many shortcuts for moving around, and it's definitely worth committing at least some of these to memory.

It's true that you can always use the mouse to drop the caret right where you need it, but this turns out to be tedious and slow. It's silly to take your hands off the keyboard, use the mouse to position the caret, and then settle back into your typing stance when it's likely you could have executed the whole process from the keyboard faster. I will start with trivial caret movement sequences you probably already know:

Keystroke	Caret Movement
↑	Up one line
↓	Down one line
←	Left one character
→	Right one character

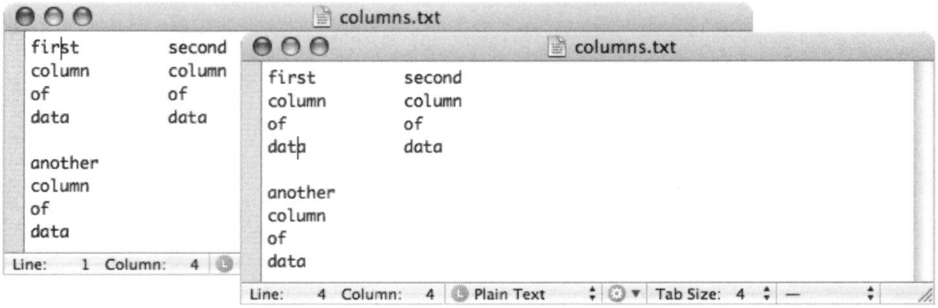

Figure 3.1: Moving to the end of the column

I'm sure those didn't surprise you, but the truth is that the simple arrows have many variations. For example, adding a ⌘ will move by lines or even to the document boundaries:

Keystroke	Caret Movement
⌘ ↑	Beginning of document
⌘ ↓	End of document
⌘ ←	Beginning of line (unaware of wrapped content)
⌘ →	End of line (unaware of wrapped content)

For smaller movements, you can use ⌥:

Keystroke	Caret Movement
⌥ ↑	Beginning of column
⌥ ↓	End of column
⌥ ←	Beginning of word
⌥ →	End of word

These column descriptions are a little tricky to grasp. When you have columns of text, you can use these shortcuts to skip all the way to the beginning or end of a column in a single keystroke. See Figure 3.1 for an example. Notice how the caret moves all the way from "first" to "data" as I press ⌥↓ in that image.

Experiment with ⌥ ← and ⌥ →. They can be helpful for moving around and making selections, which I will discuss shortly. If you often work with source code, try the variant that uses ^ instead of ⌥ and that moves between CamelCaseWords and snake_case_words.

For the emacs fans, TextMate also supports some bindings you will find familiar:

Keystroke	Caret Movement
^ P	Up one line
^ N	Down one line
^ B	Left one character
^ F	Right one character
^ A	Beginning of line (aware of wrapped content)
^ E	End of line (aware of wrapped content)
^ V	Page down

A final reason to get into the habit of using these movement functions is that the majority of them work in other Mac applications such as Mail and Safari. Learn them once, and use them everywhere.

Moving to a Line, Symbol, or Bookmark

If you are trying to get to a specific location, chances are TextMate has a shortcut that can at least get you close. For example, you can move straight to any line by number using ⌘ L. Just enter the line number in the box, and press ↵ to go there.

Being able to reach a line is great, when you know the number, but that isn't always practical. However, many of the document types Text-Mate can edit have some imposed structure. Markdown documents have header levels, for example, and source code generally involves function or method definitions. TextMate's language grammars make note of these elements so shortcuts can be provided to return to them as needed.

To access the *symbol list* via the mouse, use the pop-up menu in the lower-right corner of the editing window. Just click the header, class, method, or function to which you want to return. You can see an example of this in Figure 3.2, on the following page.

Of course, real TextMate pros would never resort to using the mouse for simple movement. To move to a symbol using the keyboard, use ⇧ ⌘ T to open the Go to Symbol dialog box from the Navigation menu. This dialog box uses the same matching algorithm described in Section 2.2, *Moving between Files*, on page 15. For example, you could enter swr to match save_without_revision(). Once your choice is highlighted, ↵ will take you straight there.

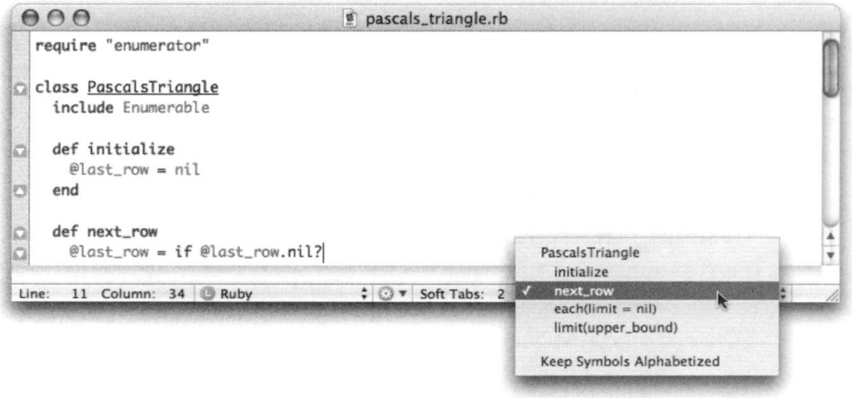

Figure 3.2: SYMBOL POP-UP MENU

If neither of those helps you get where you need to go, you can set your own *bookmarks*. To bookmark the current line, you can press ⌘F2 or click the bookmark column of the gutter, as shown in Figure 3.3, on the facing page. You must have the bookmark display active to see them in the document gutter, represented as little stars, and you can toggle this using the View → Gutter → Bookmarks (⌥⌘B). Once you have bookmarks set, you can cycle through them forward (F2) and backward (⇧F2).

Folding Sections of Code

Although *folding* isn't directly a technique for moving the caret around your document, it's much easier to make moves when you don't need to go through any extra content.

When you're working with structured content TextMate understands, you will often see folding arrows in the left margin of the editing window. Make sure View → Gutter → Foldings is checked for these to appear.

You can collapse the sections delimited by the up and down folding arrows by clicking a arrow or by pressing F1 with the caret anywhere between them in the document content. When you trigger a folding, TextMate will reduce the lines of content to a single line with an ellipsis marker at the end. The folding arrows will also be replaced with a single right-facing arrow.

If you need a glimpse of the hidden content, try mousing over the ellipsis marker, as shown in Figure 3.4, on page 26. When you are ready to

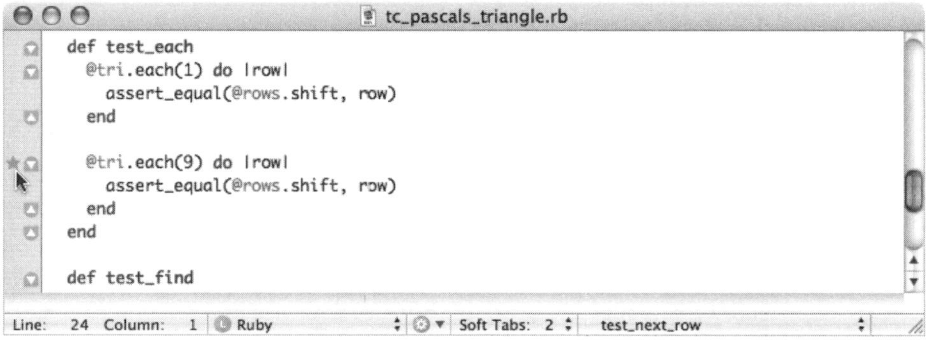

Figure 3.3: SETTING A BOOKMARK

have the content back, just click the right-facing folded arrow with the mouse, or press F1 with the caret on the folded line.

You can perform mass foldings and unfoldings using the commands under View → Toggle Foldings at Level or their keyboard equivalents. Depending on the document type, you can often use ⌥⌘2 or ⌥⌘3 to reduce the document to a high-level overview. Practice a little with the commands here to get a feel for how they might be of use to you. You can also fold or unfold a tree of nested arrows by holding down the ⌥ key as you click a folding arrow.

3.2   Making Selections

When you are ready to edit text, a common first step is to select it. With the selection you can move the content, search inside it, or filter it through commands. That's why TextMate makes selecting any amount of text as easy as possible.

First I'll tell you the good news: Everything you just learned about movement also applies to selections. If you hold down ⇧ while using the movement shortcuts (except for emacs bindings), a selection will be created, extended, or retracted from the place where the caret was to the location to which it moved. For example, to select a line (without the trailing newline), you could use the following:

1. Press ⌘→ to move the caret to the end of the line.

2. Press ⇧⌘← to move to the beginning of the line, creating a selection from the end to the beginning.

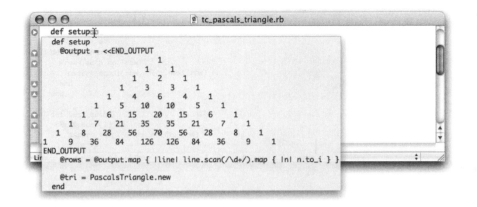

Figure 3.4: FOLDED TOOLTIP

If two steps is one too many for you, you could always reduce it to a single keystroke, as described in Chapter 7, *Macros*, on page 91. Even better, though, TextMate includes some built-in selection short-cuts including one that does the current line (with trailing newline) on ⇧ ⌘ L. My personal favorite of these is the current Word selector (^ W).

A unique option among the built-in selectors is TextMate's Current Scope selector (^ ⌥ B). This works by moving forward and backward from the caret position until the language grammar for the current document dictates that the scope would change. You can often use this to select language-specific elements. For example, you might use the scope selector to grab the contents of a string literal in a programming language as I do in Figure 3.5, on the next page.

You can find all the built-in selectors under Edit → Select. Take some time to explore the choices there so you know what's available to you the next time you need to make a selection.

Column Selections

In addition to traditional selections, TextMate allows you to work with rectangular selections or *column selections*. You can make a column selection by holding ⌥ while you drag out a selection with the mouse, or you can toggle the normal/column mode of an existing selection by pressing ⌥ or choosing Edit → Change to Column Selection.

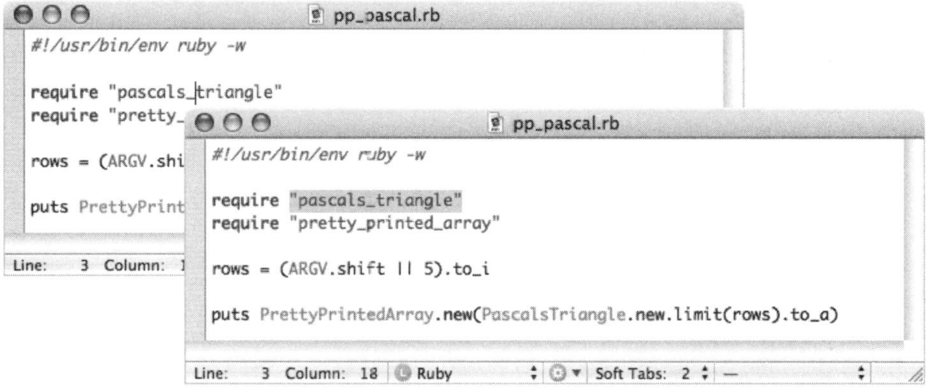

Figure 3.5: SELECT CURRENT SCOPE

You can do anything with a column selection you can with a regular selection, such as running the contents through a command. You can also type normally to replace all lines of the column selection with the same content. Here's an example that shows how to quickly generate a list of names:

1. Create a new TextMate document by choosing File → New. (⌘ N).
2. Enter some first names, each on a separate line. I used Jim↵, Marsha↵, James↵, Dana↵, and Andrew↵.
3. Press ⌘↑ to return to the beginning of the document.
4. Make a selection to the end of the column with ⇧ ⌥ ↓. It won't look like you grabbed the whole column with this move, but because you have the newline character of the next-to-last line, the selection does extend to the beginning of the last line. The difference will become clear in the next step.
5. Switch into column selection mode by tapping ⌥. You should now have a zero-width selection down the front of the lines.
6. Enter a last name such as Gray, followed by a comma and space. This will be added to all the lines of the column selection.

To leave column selection mode, move the caret to a new line.

Be warned, column selections can be surprising when used on soft-wrapped lines. Unlike some editors, TextMate does support column selections with View → Soft Wrap (⌥ ⌘ W) enabled. However, a column selection will not treat wrapped content as a new line in the selection.

You can see which lines are wrapped by looking for the dot in the left gutter of the editing window as long as View → Gutter → Soft Wrap Indicators is on. See Figure 3.7, on page 34, for a look at the soft wrap dots and how a column selection across soft-wrapped lines looks.

3.3 Editing

After you get the caret where you need it and select some content, it's time to make changes. I'll cover how to use find and replace inside a selection in Chapter 4, *Find and Replace*, on page 37 and how to call on powerful transformations in Chapter 8, *Commands*, on page 97. However, if your needs are simple, TextMate has the usual set of helpers.

Inserting New Content

TextMate has two features that are just invaluable when entering content. You'll want to get familiar with both the *completion* and *autopaired characters* features.

Completion is something you can really get a lot of mileage out of, and I need to teach you only one key. Every chance you get, start typing the first few letters of something, and press ♾. You can use this to finish off variables, methods, tags, or any other name already in your document. In addition, many grammars provide a default set of common completions for that language. This is an important habit for programmers to get into because it dramatically reduces typos.

When there is more than one completion choice, you just keep pressing ♾ to cycle through them. TextMate sorts the completion order so that matches close to your caret come up sooner, which often give it accurate results with just a couple of clicks. If you go sailing past your desired completion, you can return to it with ⇧ ♾, which reverses the cycle.

For example, let's say you are programming some manner of server. You need type a long but informative variable name such as idle_connections only the first time you use it. From then on you can try the far shorter idl♾. Depending on how many constructs in your code start with those three letters, you might need to add an extra ♾ or two to get to the desired variable, but TextMate's sorting of matches should keep the key count low. By using this technique you can guarantee you will not debug a misspelled variable name. That doesn't just apply to pro-

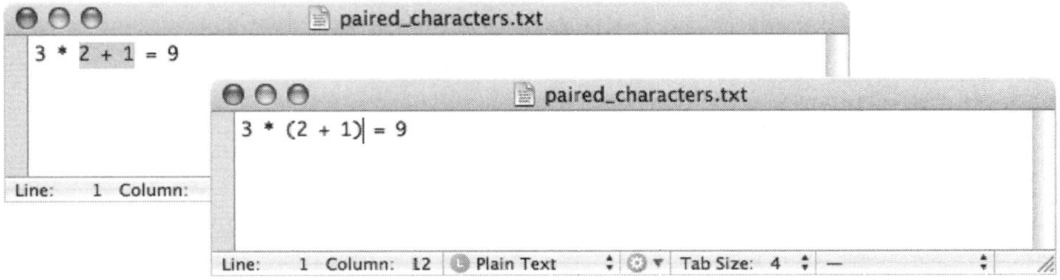

Figure 3.6: WRAPPING A SELECTION IN PAIRED CHARACTERS

gramming either; consider all the hard-to-spell names you've typed in documents over the years.

You can find the commands for completion under Edit → Completion, but this is one of those features that just makes so much more sense from the keyboard. Trust me, this is the best excuse you've ever had to wear out that ↺ key.

You've probably already run into the autopaired characters feature of TextMate if you've used it for any amount of time. In most cases, when you enter a (, TextMate also adds the closing) but leaves your caret between them. When you reach the end, you can overtype the) to get past it or use the end-of-line commands described in the Section 5.11, *The Source Bundle*, on page 74. This feature works with many commonly paired characters including quotes. Specific languages provide different paired characters, such as the helpful CSS pair that recognizes when you type a colon and adds the closing semicolon.

Another terrific way to take advantage of paired characters is with selections. If you type an opening character when some text is selected, the character will be placed at the beginning of the selection, and the matching end character will be inserted just after the selection. You can see an example of this in Figure 3.6, where I use the feature to override operator precedence. It's easy to become so fond of this feature that you are constantly destroying content in less intelligent applications.[1]

---

1. Undo is your friend when this phase sets in! Of course, the more editing you do in TextMate, the less you will run into this problem.

Moving Text

You will often need to shift contents slightly in one direction. Text → Move Selection has commands for this:

Keystroke	Caret Movement
^ ⌘ ↑	Move selection up (works on current line when nothing is selected)
^ ⌘ ↓	Move selection down (works on current line when nothing is selected)
^ ⌘ ←	Move selection left one character
^ ⌘ →	Move selection right one character

Along similar lines, TextMate makes it easy to adjust the indent level of a selection of lines using some commands found in the Text menu:

Keystroke	Indentation Change
⌘ [or ⌥ ↤	Decrease selection indent (works on current line when nothing is selected)
⌘] or ⌥ ↦	Increase selection indent (works on current line when nothing is selected)
⌥ ⌘ [	Reindent selection based on current language grammar rules (works on current line when nothing is selected)

Cut, Copy, and Paste

Another means to move text around is to use commands such as Cut, Copy, and Paste from the Edit menu. These commands are common in the majority of software these days, but TextMate gives this standard concept a twist by adding a clipboard history. Let's play around with this a little so you can get a feel for it:

1. Create a new TextMate document (⌘ N).
2. Enter these three lines of text:
   ```
   Line three.
   Line one.
   Line two.
   ```
3. So you can reorder them correctly, add them to the clipboard history in reverse order. Go to the first line of the document (⌘ ↑), select the line (⇧ ⌘ L), and cut it to the clipboard (⌘ X). Do the same with the bottom line (↓, ⇧ ⌘ L, then ⌘ X) and, finally, the last line of the document (↑, ⇧ ⌘ L, then ⌘ X).
4. Now you can paste them in order. Paste the last line you added to the history with ⌘ V. Now you want to paste the previous item from the clipboard history, and you can do that with ⇧ ⌘ V. Use

⇧ ⌘ V one last time to get the third line, and you should be looking at the lines in proper order.

Don't panic if you don't end up adding lines to the clipboard history in the perfect order. TextMate has that covered too. When you press ^ ⌥ ⌘ V or select Edit → Paste from History, TextMate will open a list of everything in the clipboard history. You then just use the arrow keys to navigate to what you want to paste and ↵ to drop it in. If you change your mind, ⟳ will dismiss the list.

An important fact to remember about pastes is that TextMate reindents them by default to match the current indention level of the document. This saves you some additional cleanup most of the time, but for the instances where you don't want the content altered there is Paste Without Re-indent. You can find this command by pressing ^ while the Edit menu is open, or you can just activate it directly from the keyboard with ^ ⌘ V. If this feature bothers you, you can disable it in the Text Editing pane of TextMate's Preferences dialog box (⌘ ,).

Editing Multiple Lines at Once

This next feature always elicits "How did you do that?" questions from people watching over my shoulder. Aside from its party trick value, though, it is genuinely useful at times.

TextMate will allow you to edit multiple lines at the same time. You can use this feature to insert new content or remove old content. This often comes in handy when working with list data.

To show this feature off properly, you need a little content to play with. That sounds like a good excuse to use TextMate to generate some.

Why don't you create a simple web page, listing computers you might use TextMate on? You will leverage TextMate's built-in HTML automations to quickly construct some tags and fill them with content. You can read more about the tools used here in Section 5.2, *The HTML and CSS Bundles*, on page 56. Follow along now:

1. Create a new TextMate document with ⌘ N.
2. Switch the language of the working document to HTML by pressing ^ ⌥ ⇧ H.
3. Now add some basic document structure. Type doctype→, and press 2 to choose HTML 4.01 (Transitional). Add the required root tag by typing html and pressing ^ <. Then press ↵ to give you some more room for content.

4. Now you need header material. Type head→, and fill in the title of *Apple Products*. Now press ↓ twice, and add a ↵ to make room for the body.

5. You can create the body section just as you did the root tag: type body, press ⌃<, and add a ↵ to split the tags.

6. Let's throw a header tag in the page. You'll switch tag creation strategies now and start with ⌃<. So, type h1 for the tag name, press →ı to jump into the content, and enter *Computers TextMate Runs On:*. Then use ⌘↵ twice to bypass the closing tag and give you some more room.

7. You're ready for the list. Start it off with ⌃<, type ul for the tag name, use →ı to skip to the content, and add a ↵ to get a blank line. Forget about tags for a moment, and enter these lines:

```
Mac mini
iMac
Mac Pro
Macbook
Macbook Pro
```

You need to select those computers so you can wrap them in tags. Start by grabbing the bottom one. With your caret right at the end of *Macbook Pro*, press ⇧⌥← twice. You can now grab the rest of the rows using ⇧⌥↑. Add a final ⇧⌥← to keep the spacing even. You can now summon all of the missing tags with ⌃⇧⌘W.

8. Time to check your hard work with ⌃⌥⌘P.

I'll talk a lot more about how you just generated more than 500 bytes of content with a little more than 100 keystrokes in Chapter 5, *Built-in Automations*, on page 53, but for now let's modify the new page. Say you decided from the preview that it would be nice to know whether a listed machine was a desktop or laptop computer. Here's how I would add the designations:

1. Press ⇧⌘L to select the current line (the first computer in our list). Hold down ⇧ so you can extend the selection, and tap ↓ twice to grab the other two desktops.

2. Select Edit Each Line in Selection from the Text menu with ⌥⌘A.

3. Press ⌥← twice to slide in front of the end tags, and enter a space followed by (desktop).

4. Use the same steps to add a space followed by (laptop) to the bottom two lines.

As you just saw, Edit Each Line in Selection allows you to add to or remove from multiple lines of content at once. It's similar in function to a column selection, save that the content doesn't need to be perfectly aligned. This generally makes it good for inserting content toward the end of a series of lines as you just did.

Changing Case

I'm sure you're used to adjusting the case of words from time to time. As usual, TextMate makes this a trivial task, often not even requiring a selection. Here are the shortcuts to the relevant commands in the Convert submenu of the Text menu:

Keystroke	Case Change
^ U	Uppercase selection (works on current word when nothing is selected)
^ ⇧ U	Lowercase selection (works on current word when nothing is selected)
^ ⌥ U	Title case each word of the selection (works on current line when nothing is selected)
^ G or ^ ⌥ G	Reverse the case of the selection (^ G works on the next character, and ^ ⌥ G works from the caret to the end of the next word when nothing is selected)

Editing Modes

TextMate supports two additional editing modes that can be useful when you are working with fixed-width data or ASCII diagrams. The modes are *Freehanded Editing* and *Overwrite Mode*, and you can find them under Edit → Mode.

When you toggle on Freehanded Editing mode (⌥ ⌘ E), TextMate will allow you to place the caret freely with keyboard arrow movement or a mouse click. You can place it beyond the ends of lines or in the middle of tabs. If you insert content, TextMate will add the needed whitespace to support the content at that location.

Note that this mode is always enabled when you are working with a column selection so you can extend them beyond the ends of lines. If you want to toggle this mode for a single mouse click, hold down ⌥ while you click.

The other editing mode, Overwrite Mode (⌥ ⌘ O), changes how TextMate behaves when the caret is in the middle of existing content. You can recognize when this mode is active because the caret will be a flat bar

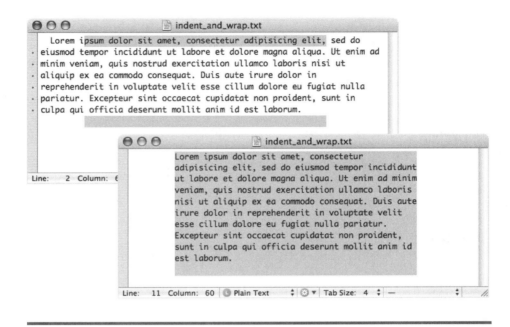

Figure 3.7: REFORMAT PARAGRAPH

under your typed content, instead of the regular insertion bar. Instead of inserting text between characters as it usually does, TextMate will replace the characters above the caret as you type. This is useful to avoid shifting later content in the line when you must replace text.

These modes can cause some automations to behave abnormally. If you see strange results when trying to activate commands, make sure these modes are turned off. They are intended for hand-editing only.

Alignment

You will find that TextMate supports the traditional suite of alignment operations with the Align submenu of the Text menu. In addition, the Text menu contains three helpful commands to fix imperfect alignments:

Keystroke	Hard Wrap Change
^Q	Reformats the current paragraph
^J	Reformats and justifies the current paragraph
^⌥Q	Unwraps the current paragraph by removing any newline characters it contains

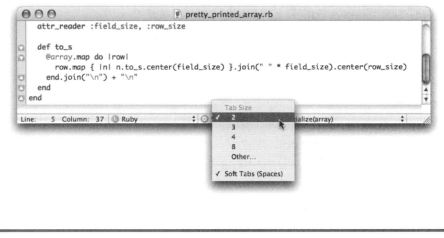

Figure 3.8: THE TAB MENU

The term *reformat* refers to the whitespace of the content, as far as these commands go. Spacing is normalized, and hard line breaks are added to wrap the content. The justify command will add extra spacing to align the right margin of the content as well.

When combined with column selections, these commands can adjust the wrap or even the indention of your content. The process is simple: Make a column selection inside the text for the dimensions you want to restrict the end result to and trigger Text → Reformat Paragraph (^ Q). Your content will be rearranged to fit your selection, as shown in Figure 3.7, on the preceding page.

Working with Tabs

You can change the current tab size using the menu embedded in the lower frame of the editing window or even enable the use of *Soft Tabs*. You can see this menu in Figure 3.8. When Soft Tabs are active, Text-Mate will still pretend you are inserting or moving past tabs, but the document will actually contain spaces when saved to disk. These settings will be remembered for all documents of the current language type.

TextMate also has a *Smart Tab* feature you have probably encountered. When you press →| at the beginning of a line, a number of tabs needed to match the indent level of the previous line will actually be inserted.

Should you need to switch to or from tabs, use Text → Convert → Spaces to Tabs and Text → Convert → Tabs to Spaces. These commands work with the selection when there is one or with the entire document when nothing is selected.

Spelling

TextMate has the standard set of spelling commands under Edit → Spelling, including the popular Check Spelling as You Type (⌥ ⌘ ;).[2] Even here, though, TextMate sneaks in an effective shortcut. When your cursor is in the middle of a misspelled word, you can open the contextual menu (as if you had clicked the mouse while holding ^) with ⌥ F2. From here you can use the arrow keys and ↵ to make corrections from the list of suggested spellings.

emacs Key Bindings

Just as you saw with the movement shortcuts, TextMate also supports some common emacs editing key bindings. Here's the list:

Keystroke	Edit
^ D	Deletes the character to the right of the caret.
^ T	Transposes the characters on either side of the caret, when there is no selection. A selection of characters will be reversed character by character and a selection of lines reversed line by line. You can find this command in the Convert submenu of the Text menu.
^ K	"Kills" all text to the end of the line.
^ Y	Yanks text back from the "kill" buffer.
^ O	Inserts a newline without moving the caret.

Again, these emacs bindings work in many Mac applications. Try them the next time you are writing an email with Apple's Mail program.

The tools described in this chapter are invaluable for focused editing in a single file, and I expect you will use them often. When you need to make more sweeping changes, though, possibly even in multiple files, you'll want a strong collection of search features. TextMate has them, and they're up next.

---

2. This command is known to slow down TextMate's performance, especially when used with long lines of text. If you must work with long lines, shut this off, and check the spelling manually with the other commands in the Spelling submenu of the Edit menu.

Chapter 4

Find and Replace

When editing text, there's no greater ally than a good set of find-and-replace tools. Filling in two quick fields and clicking a button to make a change throughout a document or even in multiple documents is far more efficient than hunting down each instance and making the change by hand. *Regular expressions*, a mini-language for describing find-and-replace operations, have become popular in text editors, Unix command-line tools, and other pieces of software used to change text.

Regular expressions are surrounded by an aura of mystery in the minds of many. I kid you not when I say that some of my colleagues are awed by those of us who can completely rework text with our mystical expressions. Some are outright afraid to try to learn what the expressions mean. To many, they are quite a mystery.

Now I'm going to let you in on a big secret: Getting started with regular expressions is easy. I've seen non–computer scientists master the basics in one evening. This chapter will take you through those initial steps. You will be amazed at the power you have just a few pages from now.

Regular expressions will help you locate and transform portions of your work, based on semi-intelligent patterns. Before you can put them to use, though, you need to examine TextMate's tools for searching, which can be helpful in their own right.

4.1 Without Using a Regular Expression

I'll get to regular expressions in just a moment, but you can perform several tasks in TextMate without them. A largely undocumented feature of TextMate is Forward Incremental Search. Mac users are probably more familiar with the term *live search* from applications such as iTunes, and in truth I think of this feature as a visual quick scan.

Scanning

Let's jump right into an example of how to use this. TextMate comes with complete release notes describing what is new and what has changed in each version of the editor. Suppose you wanted to read about the new features:

1. Select Help → Release Notes. This opens the list in a regular TextMate editing window.

2. Click ^S, and watch what happens to the bottom of the editing window when you do. The control bar that usually holds line and column counts along with language, automation, tab, and symbol menus will be replaced with a text-entry field.

3. Enter [new] in the exposed field. As soon as you begin to type, TextMate will start a selection. When you have entered the first character, the first bracket of the document will be selected. When you add the second character, TextMate will move the selection forward to select the first occurrence of the pair. Note that this scan is not case-sensitive, although scans will be when you mix case in the search string.

4. Press ^S a few more times to skip ahead in the document to subsequent matches.

5. Press ^⇧S to go backward in a document to a previous match.

6. When you are finished experimenting, press ↵ or ↺ to once again hide the scanning field.

See Figure 4.1, on the next page, for an example of how this plays out. As you can see, this is helpful for quickly scanning through document content.

The Find Dialog Box

You can summon TextMate's find-and-replace dialog box by selecting Edit → Find → Find or by pressing ⌘F. This dialog box works similarly to the one in many other Mac applications when the Regular Expression box is not checked.

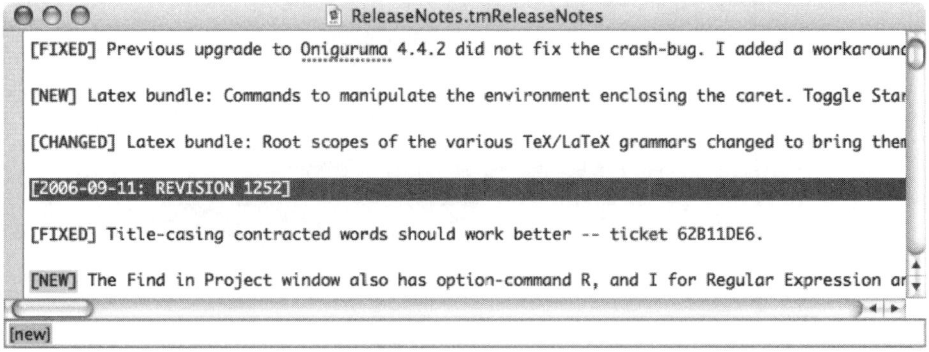

Figure 4.1: SCANNING SEARCH

You enter some text to locate in the Find field and optionally some text to replace it with in the Replace field. Because ⇥ will jump you between fields and ↵ will trigger the search, you cannot enter these characters directly. If you need them, use ⌥⇥ and ⌥↵ instead. Also note that you can expand the size of these fields with the arrow button to the right of the Replace field when you need to enter a lot of text. You can use the blue menu buttons at the end of each field to select recent entries.

Before you start a search, you can toggle the modifier checkboxes using the mouse or their ⌥⌘R, ⌥⌘I, and ⌥⌘W keyboard shortcuts. I will be talking a lot about the Regular Expression box soon, but Ignore Case causes the search to treat uppercase and lowercase characters as equal and the Wrap Around box will cause the search to return to the beginning of the document when it reaches the end.

When you have your search defined, you can fire it off with the buttons at the bottom of the window. For a simple find, use ↵ to trigger the Next button. Alternately, you can use Previous to search backward from the current caret location. I'm not a big fan of the Replace or Replace & Find buttons. The former is confusing in function, and the latter is better used outside the dialog box, which I will talk about in a moment. If you need to perform a Replace All, use the leftmost button or the key equivalent, which is ^⌘F. You can even expose a (Replace All) In Selection button by holding down ⇧, or you can just trigger that operation with ^⇧⌘F. It can be helpful to click the Σ (a summation operator in math) button to the right of the Find field before using the Replace All buttons. It will show a count in the dialog box of how many matches it finds. See Figure 4.2, on the following page for an example.

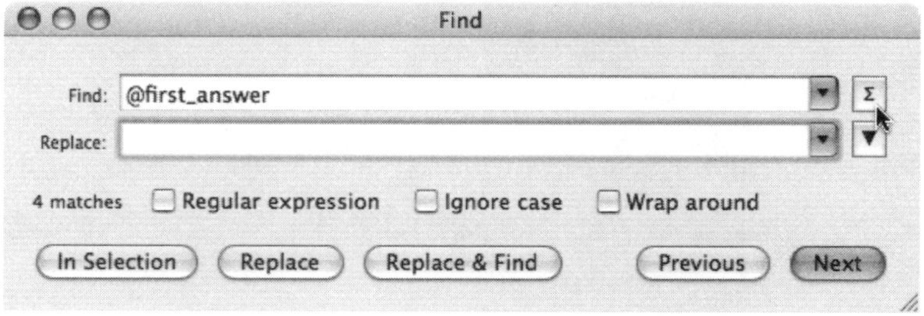

Figure 4.2: COUNTING MATCHES

It's important to note that this process can often be driven from the keyboard without ever opening the dialog box; you just need to press the key equivalents for the commands in the Edit → Find. Use ⌘ E to place the current selection in the Find field,[1] ⌘ G to find the next occurrence, and ⌥ ⌘ F to replace the selected occurrence and locate the next, for example. You can also use ⇧ ⌘ E to place the current selection, or an empty string if there is no selection, in the Replace field.

Find in Project

When you want to make changes to many files at once, you can access a similar dialog box by selecting Edit → Find → Find in Project (⇧ ⌘ F). Most of the controls here work just as they did for the find-and-replace dialog box, although the dialog itself looks somewhat different.

After setting up your search details, use ↵ to kick off the find process. TextMate will find all matches in your project and show them in the lower half of the dialog box. You can click any of these matches to go to the match in the indicated file.

One great element of a project search is your choice for replacement. After a project find, you can use the Replace All button to make the change in each place shown. However, if you need to handpick the replacements, you can do that as well. Select matches in the lower half of the window using the mouse. You can hold ⇧ while you click to select entire ranges or ⌘ to add or remove individual matches. When

---

1. This handy trick works in most Mac applications, not just TextMate. It's also helpful to know that these applications share a find clipboard, so using ⌘ E in one really updates them all.

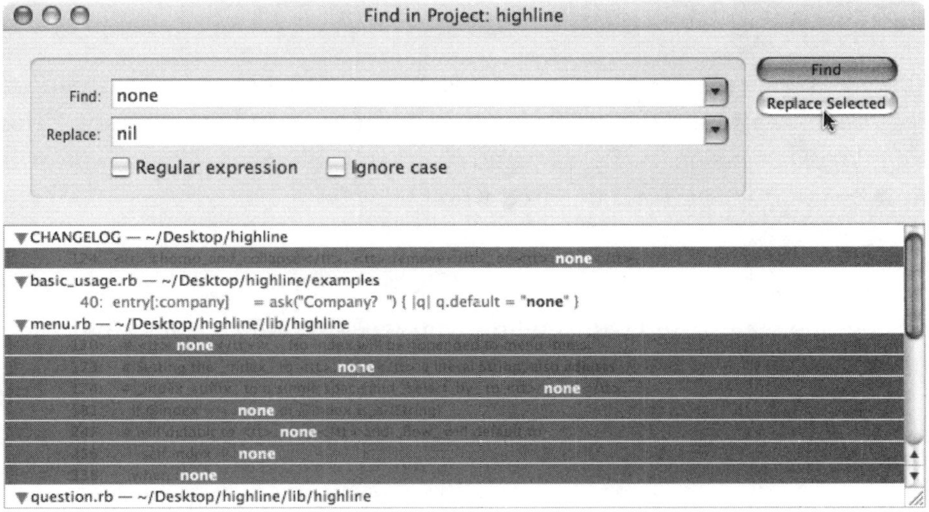

Figure 4.3: REPLACE SELECTED BUTTON

you have selected all the matches you want to change, click the Replace Selected button to change just those. You can see this process in action in Figure 4.3.

Searching an entire project can take time. If you are interested only in matching certain files, it's often a good idea to limit the search to just those files. You can do this in TextMate using a new project. Fill it with the files you are interested in, do the search, and then discard the project. You can often build these projects quickly with the help of mate. For example, if I want to build a project of just the Ruby source code files in the lib and test directories, I navigate to the directory just above those with the Terminal and enter this:

```
$ find {lib,test} -name '*.rb' -print0 | xargs -0 mate
```

You can do the same with the mouse, if you prefer. Just drag a collection of selected files or folders down to the Dock, and drop them on TextMate's icon. This tells TextMate to build a new project containing just what you dropped.

When the project opens, I can perform my project search and then close the project. This limits the search to only where I need it and generally speeds things up.

4.2 Mixing in Regular Expressions

You've now seen the two Find dialog boxes and how to use them in regular operations. You also saw that both dialog boxes included the Regular Expression checkbox, and when you flip that switch, you will now be conducting searches in a whole new language.

TextMate uses the *Oniguruma* regular expression engine. This is a full-featured and fast library for working with regular expressions. If you are familiar with the PCRE engine, you will be glad to know that they have similar capabilities and syntax.

In a regular expression, the characters you type describe what you are searching for so that TextMate can locate it for you. You are able to specify things such as the kinds of characters you want to find, how many of them, and possible alternatives you will accept in a match. You provide this description using characters that have special meanings within a regular expression.

Special Characters

In fact, you already know more than you might think about regular expressions. A few characters have special meaning in the expression, but everything else matches just as it would in a regular search. Put another way, most characters match themselves. An E in a regular expression will match a capital *E* literally.

Here are the special characters inside an expression:

```
\ . [ ] ^ $ ? * + { } ( ) |
```

All other characters retain their regular meanings when used in a regular expression. That means the expression James will locate my name, <p> will match paragraph tags in HTML, and 4 - 2 = 3 will check the document for one possible erroneous math expression.

Should you need to use a special character as a literal match in a regular expression, just precede the character with a backslash (\) to *escape* it. Using this, you could hunt through a document for all payments of exactly 100 U.S. dollars with the expression \$100.

You are welcome to use literal tabs and newline characters in an expression, but it's often easier to enter them as \t or \n to keep the expression compact and avoid triggering controls on TextMate's Find dialog boxes. These shortcuts work in TextMate's replacement strings as well.

Character Classes

Sometimes you don't want to match exact characters. Sometimes any one of a list of characters will do, and in a regular expression you can use a *character class* to specify this.

Character classes are surrounded with brackets ([...]), and they indicate all the characters you will accept where they occur in the match. For example, the expression [aeiou] will match a single English vowel, the expression [\t] will match a space or tab character, and the expression [cbr]at will find the animals cat, bat, or rat.

It's important to note that the latter expression will not find the entire word *brat*. It would only select the *rat* inside the word, leaving the *b* untouched. Character classes just match one letter but give multiple choices for what that letter can be.

Most special characters listed in Section 4.2, *Special Characters*, on the facing page revert to their regular meanings inside a character class. The expression [$()|] will match a dollar sign, an opening or closing parenthesis, or a vertical bar. Inside character classes, the caret (^), hyphen (-), and backslash (\) have special meanings.

Instead of listing what's acceptable in a character class, you are allowed to list what is not acceptable. If the first character of a character class is a caret (^), the meaning is reversed, and it will match anything not listed. Therefore, the expression [^aeiou] will match the first nonvowel character it finds. That might be a consonant; a whitespace character such as a space, tab, or newline; a Greek letter; some symbol; or anything else. If you need to use a literal caret (^) in a character class, place it anywhere but as the first character, or escape it with a leading backslash (\).

Character classes can include ranges of characters. To provide a range, give the first character in the sequence, a hyphen (-), and the final character of the sequence. The three most common uses of this are to match the following:

```
[a-z]  Any lowercase English letter
[A-Z]  Any uppercase English letter
[0-9]  Any digit
```

You can have multiple ranges in a class, so the expression [a-zA-Z] matches lowercase and uppercase letters. Ranges work based on the ordering of characters in the current encoding, so I don't recommend using them for anything other than letters or numbers. If you need to use a literal hyphen (-) in a character class, make it the first character of the class, or escape it with a leading backslash (\). Remember to escape brackets ([]) by proceeding them with a backslash (\) if you are trying to include literal brackets in a character class.

Finally, you can use several shortcut character classes in a regular expression without the brackets:

```
.   Any character except a newline
\s  Any whitespace character including space, tab, and newline
\S  Any nonwhitespace character
\w  A word character, equivalent to [a-zA-Z0-9_]
\W  A nonword character, equivalent to [^a-zA-Z0-9_]
\d  A digit, equivalent to [0-9]
\D  A nondigit, equivalent to [^0-9]
```

You can even use all of those except the period (.) inside a character class to combine with other characters. For example, [\w'] matches a word character or apostrophe, and [\d,] matches a digit or comma.

Anchors

Regular expressions can be pretty generous in what they accept. For example, the expression ship will match *ship*, *ships*, *worship*, and a lot more. Anything containing that sequence of letters is a match.

What if you really wanted just the word *ship*, though? You could add a space to either end of the expression, and that would keep it from matching words such as *ships* and *worship*. However, if the word *ship* is the very first thing in a document, it won't have a space in front of it, and you would fail to match it.

In regular expressions, you can solve these problems with *anchors*. Here's a list of the commonly used anchors:

```
^   Matches at the beginning of any line
$   Matches at the end of any line
\b  Matches between \w\W or \W\w sequences and at the beginning
    or end of document
\B  Matches anywhere \b does not
\A  Matches at the beginning of the input
\Z  Matches at the end of the input or just before the final newline
\z  Matches at the end of the input
```

Note that these are all zero-width assertions that do not consume any characters of the input. They simply restrict where a match can occur. You now have the information you need to improve the earlier attempt to match just the word *ship*. Using the word boundary assertion, you can modify the expression to \bship\b. Similarly, you could match a digit at the end of the line with \d$ and check to see whether a TextMate document begins with a Unix shebang line using \A#!.

Quantifiers

So far I've talked a lot about specifying what you want to match. An equally common concern of regular expressions is how much of it you want to match. For that, I need to talk about the *quantifiers*. Here's the list:

```
?       Zero or one
*       Zero or more
+       One or more
{n}     Exactly n
{n,}    At least n
{,n}    No more than n
{n,m}   At least n, but no more than m
```

In the previous list, n and m represent positive integers.

You place the quantifier after the element you want to repeat, so [aeiou]+ matches one or more vowels, \d{5} matches five consecutive digits, and \bships?\b matches ship or ships.

All quantifiers are greedy by default, which means they will consume as many characters as they can without causing the match to fail. I'll now show an example of that:

1. Create a new TextMate document (⌘ N).
2. Enter the content abbcbbbbbc.
3. Place your cursor at the beginning of the document (⌘ ↑), and open the Find dialog box (⌘ F).
4. Switch to Regular Expression if needed (⌥ ⌘ R), and enter the expression a.+c in the Find field.
5. Click Next (↵) to perform the search.

TextMate should select the entire line, skipping over the first c to consume as many characters as possible. That's what I mean by *greedy*.

Try the same experiment one more time, but use a pattern of a.+?c instead. Now TextMate should select only to the first c. Adding a question mark (?) to the end of a quantifier modifies it to match the fewest possible characters.

It's important to remember that the quantifiers affect only the element just before them in the expression. This means that the expression ho+ will match *ho, hoo, hooo*, and so on, but it will not match *hoho*. For that, you need another tool.

Grouping and Capturing

Parentheses ((...)) serve two purposes in a regular expression. First, they *group* elements. Using that information, you could build an expression that matches repeating words instead of just characters. For example, the expression (ho)+ matches *ho, hoho, hohoho*, and so on. Similarly, you could shorten an expression to match a typical IP address:

```
Without grouping:   \b\d{1,3}\.\d{1,3}\.\d{1,3}\.\d{1,3}\b
With grouping:      \b\d{1,3}(\.\d{1,3}){3}\b
```

The other feature of parentheses ((...)) is to *capture* sections of a match. This is commonly used in replacement strings to insert pieces of the match inside the new string. Let's see an example of this in action:

1. Create a new document (⌘ N).
2. Type Gray,James.
3. Move to the beginning of the document (⌘ ↑), and open the Find dialog box (⌘ F).
4. Make sure you are in Regular Expression mode (⌥ ⌘ R).
5. Enter the expression (\w+),\s*(\w+) in the Find field, and set the Replacement to {:first => "$2", :last => "$1", :full => "$2 $1"}.
6. Trigger the change with the Replace All button (^ ⌘ F).

The expression dissects the name, and TextMate uses the captures in the replacement string to properly identify the first and last names. It also combines the captures to create a full name.

As you just saw, you can access the contents of parenthetical captures in a replacement string with the variables $1, $2, and so on. $1 points to the leftmost capture, $2 points to the capture following that one from left to right, $3 points to the next one, and so on. Therefore, you could use an expression such as ^(([^:\n]+):(.+))$ to match email-style headers and later access the entire line in $1, the header name in $2, and the header contents in $3.

You can even access captures from earlier in the match inside the match itself. You do this using *back references*, which are similar to replacement variables but with a backslash (\) in front of the numeral.

For example, if you need a single- or double-quoted string in a document, you might use a pattern such as (["']).*?\1. This will match *"James"* or *'James'* but not *"James'* since the second quote is a back reference to the first matched quote.

If you want to group some elements but don't need to capture them, you can use a slight variation of the parentheses ((?:...)). For example, to match a run of words, you might use something like ((?:\w+\s*)+). The individual words are not captured by that expression, but the entire phrase will be in $1 as usual.

Alternation

Another option of regular expressions is to specify choices of what can appear at a given point in the expression using *alternation*. Each option can be a complete *subexpression*, allowing for more complex choices than a class of characters. Choices are separated with a vertical bar (|). Thus, you can move through your document by runs of word and nonword characters by running a find for the expression \w+|\W+ and using ⌘G to jump to each successive match.

Unlike most regular expression operators, the vertical bar (|) does not apply to just the previous element of the match. It applies to the entire subexpression before and after. In other words, the expression TODO[:,]\s*|--\S.* will match a TODO tag followed by a colon or comma and some optional whitespace, or it will match two hyphens followed by some content. Notice how the second half has nothing to do with a TODO tag. You can limit the alternation operation using grouping, so we could fix the previous expression to what was more likely intended with TODO([:,]\s*|--)\S.*.

For example, you may want to match a quoted string that can contain nested quotes, as long as they are escaped. This means the string could contain nonquote, nonbackslash characters; escaped quotes (\"); or escaped literal backslashes (\\). You can express those options with alternation ("(\\\\|\\"|([^"\\]+))+").

Advanced Features

This book isn't big enough for me to cover all the advanced features supported by Oniguruma,[2] but I want to hit a few highlights before I wrap this up.

---

2. See the official documentation at http://www.geocities.jp/koscko3/oniguruma/doc/RE.txt if you want to learn more.

First, you will want to be aware that regular expressions have *modes*. Two of the most common modes to use are the mode for case-insensitive matching and the mode for multiline processing. You can turn these on for a portion of your expression by wrapping your subexpression in (?i:...) for case-insensitive matching or (?m:...) for multiline matching. The effect of the former is just what you expect from the name; the expression (?i:james) will match *james*, *James*, *JAMES*, or even *jAmEs*. For the latter mode, the period (.) is modified to match any character, including newlines. Using that, the expression (?m:.{10}) matches the first ten characters, even if they span multiple lines. I'll discuss a third mode in Section 10.1, *Documenting a Grammar*, on page 146.

Another powerful feature of some regular expression engines, including Oniguruma, is *look-around assertions*. These are zero-width assertions that allow you to peek forward or backward in the input without consuming characters. You might use this to verify that some input is present but keep it out of the matched data. For example, the expression (?<=<li>)(?m:.*?)(?=</li>) will match simple list item tags in an HTML document, selecting only the content of the tag, not the tag itself. Here's a complete list of the look-around assertions:

```
(?=...)    Look-ahead
(?!...)    Negative look-ahead
(?<=...)   Look-behind
(?<!...)   Negative look-behind
```

TextMate has a few additional features for replacement strings. You can change the case of text in a replacement string by using *case foldings*. This is quite useful when you use the variables to access content from the match. To uppercase or lowercase the next character in the replacement, use \u or \l. To affect a run of characters, surround them in \U...\E or \L...\E. For example, I can use the expression \b(?i:(james))\b to find my first name in any state of capitalization, and I can use this replacement \u\L$1\E string to ensure that it is title cased after the replacement.

The other feature TextMate exposes in replacement strings is the ability to do *conditional replacement*. You can optionally add content to the replacement if a capture variable contains any matched data. The syntax for this is to wrap the replacement text in (?n:...) where n is the match group number to check for content. If the group holds any text, the section will be inserted; otherwise, it is discarded. You might use this to prepare a phrase for use as a variable name in a programming language using an expression such as (\w+)|(\W+) and a replacement of (?1:\L$1\E)(?2:_). That turns the title of this book, *TextMate: Power Editing for the Mac*, into *textmate_power_editing_for_the_mac*.

The search tools round out our exploration of what you can accomplish with TextMate. The real power of TextMate, though, comes from what it can accomplish for you. The next part of this book is all about that.

Part II

Automations

Chapter 5

Built-in Automations

Soon you will learn to build any TextMate automation your heart desires, but first let's get a feel for what is possible by working with some of the built-in automations. TextMate currently ships with more than thirty *bundles*—a convenient grouping of related automations. In this chapter, you will look at bundles for different languages and activities. I don't have space to cover all of them in detail, but I will hit the highlights of many of the most popular bundles.

Bundles are directories of related files packaged on your hard drive. However, from day to day, you will interact with bundles from inside TextMate using either the Bundles menu or the shortcut automation menu with the small gear icon at the bottom of every editing window. Use ⌃↺ to open the gear menu, navigate with the arrow keys, and select an item by pressing ↵.

It's important to know that bundle contents are available only when an editing window is open. This is a limitation of TextMate, even for commands that don't need a specific file on which to operate. If you go into the Bundles menu and find everything disabled, you probably just need to open a file. This issue will be addressed in a future version of TextMate.

5.1 The TODO Bundle

The TODO bundle consists of only two commands: Help and Show TODO List. The Help command describes Show TODO List. It's common for bundles to include a Help command like this, so be sure to look for them when you are exploring on your own. Take a moment to read that brief text now, and then I'll show you some additional tricks.

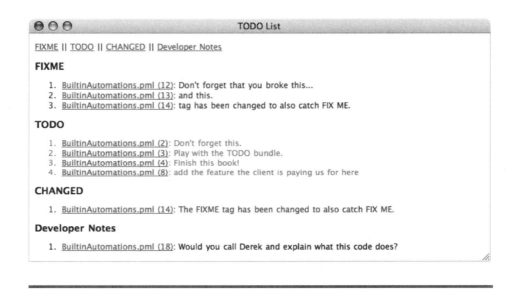

Figure 5.1: SHOW TODO LIST OUTPUT

The Show TODO List command (^⇧T) is where the action is. When invoked, all files in the current project (or the current file if working outside a project) are saved, and TextMate starts scanning for tags. The tags the command looks for can have a couple of formats:

```
TODO Don't forget this.
TODO, Play with the TODO bundle.
TODO:  Finish this book!
```

It's also important to note that the tag doesn't have to be the first thing on the line. That allows you to hide TODO items in the comments of a programming language. For example:

```
# TODO:  add the feature the client is paying us for here
```

The command isn't limited to TODO tags either:

```
FIXME:  Don't forget that you broke this...
FIX ME:  and this.
CHANGED:  The FIXME tag has been changed to also catch FIX ME.
```

When invoked, these tags are located, sorted by type, color-coded, and hyperlinked back to the line of the file where they were found. The result appears in TextMate's HTML output window. You can see what I mean in Figure 5.1, which shows the output of the tag examples in this chapter.

Joe Asks...

What Happens When My Brain Is Full?

I'm sure you remember that spirited pep talk I gave early in the book about learning your keyboard shortcuts, and I really do mean that. Everyone has their limit of what they can effectively remember, though, and no matter what your limit is, this chapter will likely exceed it. I cover twelve bundles in these pages, and that's just a fraction of what comes with TextMate. That's a lot of automations, and I throw around keyboard shortcuts for all of them. Keep the shrink bills low, and be selective about what you actually commit to memory.

First, you may not need all these bundles. If you never build web applications with Rails, for example, feel free to skip that bundle. Don't skip TODO, Math, Text, Source, or TextMate, though, because I think they might surprise you.

Next, when you do find a bundle worth committing to memory, decide what level of attention it deserves. Is this a I-will-use-it-five-times-an-hour batch of commands? OK, spend the effort learning the keyboard shortcuts. However, you can still get mileage out of a bundle without knowing the shortcut. I use the TODO bundle often, but I had to look up the keyboard shortcut to add it to this chapter. That's just because the TODO hunting mode of my workflow is a mousy action, so I don't need to memorize the shortcut. Decide when you can and can't get away with the same.

Also, be sure to notice the patterns in TextMate's shortcuts. They are there on purpose. ⌃Q is always reformat in the current context; ⌘B and ⌘I are bold and italics anywhere that makes sense; ⏎ is continue list, comment, or whatever; and ⌃⌥⌘P is how you get a preview. The bundles have a lot more patterns than that. Learn them once, and use them everywhere.

Finally, you can hunt for a command just as I've trained you to do for files and symbols. ⌃⌘T will open a dialog box with the now-famous name-matching algorithm for bundle commands. Use as needed, but if you go after the same command three times in one day, I say it's time to learn that shortcut!

The TODO bundle is helpful with what you have seen so far, but the real power lies in how easily you can add your own tags to the mix. For example, the company I work for often embeds notes to the developers in the source code we write. A note is always tagged by the intended developer's first name. I can modify the Show TODO List command to pick up those notes with a few easy steps:

1. Open the Bundle Editor (^ ⌥ ⌘ B).
2. Click the folding arrow to the left of the TODO bundle's name to expose the bundle's contents.
3. Click Show TODO List so you can see the source in the Edit Command box.
4. Add a line like the following in the $tags = [...] definition right at the beginning of the script:

```
{ :label  => "Developer Notes",
  :color  => "#0090C8",
  :regexp => /JAMES[-\s,:]+(\w.*)$/i },
```

That will find the developer note tags used by my company, as long as they are addressed to me. I've added the ability to place hyphens after the tag as well, since we tend to do just that. These tags will turn a light blue, but you could modify the HTML color code to get your favorite hue. Here's a sample note from my company found by the addition we made to the command:

```
# JAMES--Would you call Derek and explain what this code does?
```

5.2 The HTML and CSS Bundles

The HTML bundle is TextMate's most popular bundle. So many people need to create a quick web page, and HTML is an easy markup language to learn. Even still, the markup can get repetitive, and we humans tend to make mistakes when dealing with such languages—well, only those humans who don't use TextMate as their editor, that is.

If you are going to learn only one command from the HTML bundle, definitely make it Insert Open/Close Tag (With Current Word). I'm not exaggerating when I say that command, available in any document via ^ <, is 90% of what you need to write HTML, XHTML, or even XML quickly and effectively. I wrote this book primarily with that one command.

You can use Insert Open/Close Tag in two ways. First, you can type a tag name—html, div, or a, for example—and then trigger the command. The tag name will be transformed into an open and close tag pair. This

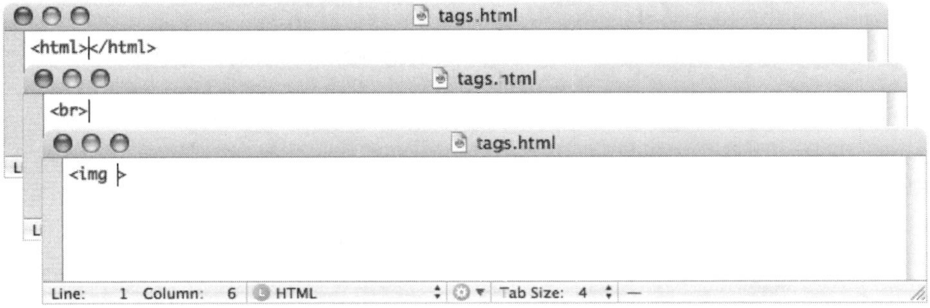

Figure 5.2: INSERT OPEN/CLOSE TAG

command is super smart, knowing to handle words like br and img with a single tag. It also always tries to drop your caret in the most logical place you need to be next. See Figure 5.2, and note the caret positions.

The other way to use the command is equally handy. Just invoke it with no word to the left of the caret, and it will generate and insert an open and close tag pair snippet. You can then type a name for the tag that will update both ends of the pair. Feel free to add tag attributes as needed, and know that they will not be copied to the closing tag. When you are ready, just press →| to jump into the content portion of the tag.

Experiment a little with both forms before reading on so you can get a good feel for the command. The two uses are handy in different contexts, and you are well armed if you know both.

Two other commands are helpful for quickly building tags: Wrap Selection in Open/Close Tag (^ ⇧ W) and Wrap Each Selected Line in Open/Close Tag (^ ⇧ ⌘ W). They both do what their names suggest, adding open and close tag pairs in front of and behind the entire selection or at the start and end of each line in the selection. You can then type a tag name that will be mirrored to all inserted instances. These commands are nice for naturally typing several paragraphs or list items without stopping to worry about syntax and then marking them up after the fact.

Of course, the HTML bundle has many other commands. Among them are some snippets for inserting tags that commonly need a little extra baggage you don't want to have to type all the time. Good examples are Head, Style, and Script. Try typing head→| in an HTML document to see what I mean. It will insert a content-type tag and set you up to edit the document title. You trigger the other two snippets I mentioned the same way (style→ or script→), and all snippets of this kind are available in the Insert Tag submenu of the HTML bundle.

I just don't have the room to explain all the excellent helpers hiding in the HTML bundle, but I'll close this section with a few more quick tips:

- Wrap Selection as Link (^ ⇧ L) works like the other wrap commands I discussed, but it will use the clipboard contents as the uniform resource locator (URL) for the link, assuming the clipboard contains a single line of text.
- For effortless linking, select the link text, and trigger Lookup Selection on Google and Link (^ ⇧ ⌘ L). This command uses Google's "I'm Feeling Lucky" to find the first match in the search list and builds a hyperlink to that site.
- Type doctype→ at the beginning of your document to select one of those hard-to-remember statements.
- Type ⌘ & for a menu of several useful commands involving entity and URL escapes.
- The common Mac shortcuts ⌘ B and ⌘ I work in HTML documents to create strong and em(phasis) tags.
- Use Window → Show Web Preview (^ ⌥ ⌘ P) to check the result of your markup work with live updating, or use the Open Document in Running Browser(s) and Refresh Running Browser(s) (⌘ R) commands in the HTML bundle to manage an external preview.
- Use Validate Syntax (W3C), available via ^ ⇧ V, to ensure that your markup is free from errors.

You can see an example using several of the HTML automations to build a web page with minimal effort in Section 3.3, *Editing Multiple Lines at Once*, on page 31.

Adding Style

TextMate makes the CSS bundle available when you're editing a style sheet or even if you are just inside a style tag in an HTML document. CSS is not complex enough to require a powerful command suite like the HTML bundle has, but the bundle still has some useful snippets.

The hard part of CSS work, in my opinion, is remembering all the combinations of what goes after a given identifier. For example, after the margin identifier, you can put one argument to set all four margins; two to set vertical and horizontal margins; or four to set top, right, bottom, and left individually. Just to write that last sentence, though, I had to look up the order. I never remember it.

That's how TextMate can help you with CSS work. It remembers all the combinations. To get it to remind you, just trigger the menus. You can do that by typing a word like background, border, font, list, margin, padding, or text, followed by →ı in a style sheet or style tag. The menu will have all the common choices, and inserting one will include placeholders that prompt you for what to fill in at each point.

If you also have as much trouble remembering HTML color codes as I do, you will be happy to hear that the CSS bundle covers those too. You can choose Bundle → CSS → Insert Color (⇧ ⌘ C), and TextMate will display the standard Mac color chooser and allow you to make a choice. The color you select is converted to the expected string of six hexadecimal digits with a leading number sign and inserted at the caret position.

5.3 The Ruby Bundle

Because TextMate's own automations use Ruby heavily, TextMate has great support for the language via a full set of automations in the Ruby bundle.

The first thing you need in Ruby support is a way to run your scripts. TextMate ships with the RubyMate runtime environment invoked by Bundles → Ruby → Run (⌘ R in any Ruby document). This hands your code off to Ruby and displays program output in TextMate's HTML output window. Before the hand-off, though, TextMate modifies the standard Ruby environment to include some nice tie-ins to the graphical user interface (GUI). TextMate arranges to be notified of uncaught exceptions and hyperlinks the stack trace output back to the lines of your file. STDIN is also modified, so a call to gets() will trigger a GUI dialog box that sends your input down to the script. The environment even detects when you are running tests so it can color-code those results and hyperlink errors and failures.

RubyMate is great for running entire scripts, but Rubyists, spoiled by the ease of IRb, often want to evaluate some little snippet and see the results. You could switch to the Terminal and use IRb itself, but TextMate provides another option. When you run Bundles → Ruby → Execute and Update '# =>' Markers, TextMate filters the selected code, or the entire document in the event of no selection, through a script. That script updates # => markers you have placed at the ends of lines with the results of that expression. You can insert such a marker using a snippet bound to #→|. The script will also annotate errors and show content printed to STDOUT. This is powerful tool for quick localized debugging or testing. For example, filtering the following code through the command:

```
RUBY_VERSION  # =>

data    = %w[one two three four five]
results = data.select { |n| n[0] == ?t }  # =>
```

yields the following:

```
RUBY_VERSION  # => "1.8.4"

data    = %w[one two three four five]
results = data.select { |n| n[0] == ?t }  # => ["two", "three"]
```

The majority of the Ruby bundle focuses on writing code, not running it. Many snippets exist for building Ruby code quickly. The good news is that the tab triggers follow mnemonic patterns to make them easier to remember.

When you are ready to create a new Ruby class or module, just press cla→| or mod→| for a menu of common skeletons. You can use a similar trigger for methods on def→|, or you can use the variations defs→| for a class or module method and deft→| for a test method. The tab triggers r→|, w→|, and rw→| are shortcuts for Ruby's attr_reader(), attr_writer(), and attr_accessor() helpers. The snippets continue all the way down to simple language constructs available on triggers such as if→|, case→|, and while→|. Get into the habit of using these, and you will never need to type **end** again.

Probably the most widely used Ruby snippets are in the iterator family of snippets. Again, the tab triggers follow patterns to make them easy to remember. Specifically, one-word iterators are available via the first three letters of the word, so inj→| will trigger inject(), and tim→| will trigger times(). The exception is each(), which uses the common abbreviation for the word ea→|. If the iterator has more than one word, add the first letter of each additional word to the trigger, so sorb→| activates sort_by() and eawi→| activates each_with_index(). Though they may seem odd now, you will learn the patterns pretty fast with practice and will seldom need to look up snippet triggers again.

Note that all the snippets use the braces syntax and that there are no snippets for the "bang" variations. You can use two commands inside an iterator body to change it to the desired variation: Add ! to Method in Line (^ !) and Toggle 'do ... end' / '{ ... }' (^ {).

TextMate provides a similar suite of snippets for unit testing. You can build a skeleton test case file with tc→ or a test suite file with ts→. All the assertions work just like the iterators, building off the base of as→ for assert(), so you can trigger assert_in_delta() with asid→, for example.

Two facts to know about the automations in the Ruby bundle are that some of them insert requires for the needed standard library files when triggered, unless your document already has the require, of course, and some are based on fictional method names to make them easier to remember. You can suppress the autorequire behavior by adding - to the tab trigger. Both eas→ and eas-→ will insert an each_slice() snippet, but the first will make sure the current document requires the enumerator library. Examples of fictional methods include map_with_index(), class_from_name(), and word_wrap(), which all insert common idioms of Ruby code to handle these operations.

Finally, the bundle provides Documentation for Word (^ H) for easy access to Ruby's built-in documentation. Just place your caret in the word you want to look up, and then trigger the command for a hyperlinked HTML response.

5.4 The Rails Bundle

The Rails core team has done a good job of advertising TextMate in its screencasts, so it's not surprising that TextMate has become a favored choice for building Rails applications. Attracting all those Rails developers has also attracted some terrific automations for the Rails bundle.

To use the Rails bundle, you need to give TextMate the hint that you are a Rails developer. You need to do this because Rails files look like regular Ruby files to TextMate. When you have a Ruby file open, glance down at the language menu embedded in the bottom of the editing window. If that menu says *Ruby*, the Rails bundle isn't yet active. To kick it into gear, select Ruby on Rails from that same menu. In Rails mode, you have access to all the Ruby goodies plus the entire Rails bundle.

For an added boost to TextMate Rails development, I recommend installing the TextMate Footnotes plugin. This plugin will add links to the pages of your application under development mode that you can click to jump right to that file in TextMate for editing. There are also links to display the parameters and session inline in the page. All are helpful and won't affect your code when it is running in production mode.

To ask TextMate to add this functionality to your Rails project, open your project, select Bundles → Rails → Install Plugin (^ I and press 2), type footnotes into the plugin search field, and click the Go button (↵). Then click the download arrow button to the far right of the TextMate Footnotes match to install the plugin.

The Rails bundle includes timesaving automations for working with each layer of a Rails application. With models, the bundle has many snippets for validations and association methods such as has_one() and belongs_to(). You can find these snippets in the Models submenu of the Rails bundle. They have mnemonic tab triggers similar to those in the Ruby bundle.

My favorite feature of the Rails bundle's model layer is the support for migrations. Here again you have some snippets for quick entry, but the tab triggers are well thought out to maximize productivity. To see what I mean, assume you have a typical create table migration started with the following:

```
create_table :favorites do |t|

end
```

Now you're ready to add a handful of columns, so you put your caret in the table block and type mccc→ to trigger Create Several Columns:

```
create_table :favorites do |t|
  t.column :user_id, :integer
  mccc
end
```

Notice how that snippet sets up entry and drops in the trigger again for the next column. There is even a tab stop right after that mccc, so you will naturally end up there. When you are about to enter the last column, just tap ⌫ a couple of times, and add an ol before triggering the snippet. This mcol→ trigger will open a menu of column creation choices from which you can select Create Column in Table by pressing 9. Then you won't have the trailing snippet trigger to clean up.

A couple of the migrations are even smarter. Drop/Create Table (mtabt→, choice 6) and Remove/Add Column (mcol→, choice 8) will insert regular snippets for the change, with special triggers at the end to kick off macros. When the macros are triggered, your db/schema.rb file will be scanned by the bundle for the details of the table or column changed. Those details are reinserted as the migration's down() action so the table or column will be restored to its former state.

With views, the shortcut to master is ^>. When you trigger that snippet, you get <%= %>; however, pressing it again accesses a command that switches the tag to <% %>. This pair of automations is actually located in the Ruby bundle, but they are commonly used to edit the RHTML files of Rails projects.

Another nice view helper is Create Partial from Selection (^ ⇧ H). You can use it, as the name implies, to separate a selection of code into a new partial file and insert a render() call to that file, but that's not all. If you invoke it without a selection, it will read all partial render() calls in the current document and inline the full partial just below each call. You can edit the contents of these documents and trigger the command again to return them to their files. See Figure 5.3, on the next page, for an example of how this plays out.

Controller work in the Rails bundle benefits from nice snippets for renders and redirects. Again, the triggers are mnemonic, and you can explore these snippets under Bundles → Rails → Controllers. Don't miss the params[...] (^ P) and session[...] (^ J) snippets in the top-level of the Rails bundle, because single-keystroke access is nice for those terms you type repeatedly.

Another challenge with Rails development is quickly navigating to the file you need to edit now. The Rails bundle adds some terrific shortcuts for this. I recommend committing one to memory. ⌥ ⇧ ⌘ ↓ will open a menu where you can select to jump to a Controller, Helper, Functional Test, Unit Test, View, or more. That makes getting around a breeze with just one shortcut to remember. Be sure to look in the Go To submenu of the Rails bundle, though, for other interesting navigation commands.

5.5   The Subversion Bundle

Most people have come to understand the value of version control, and if you're going to use version control these days, Subversion is a popular choice.[1] When you have a Subversion repository checked out, TextMate has a bundle of features that can help you get the most out of it.

---

1.   If you are not yet familiar with Subversion, *Pragmatic Version Control Using Subversion* by Mike Mason (Pragmatic Bookshelf, 2005) is a great way to get started.

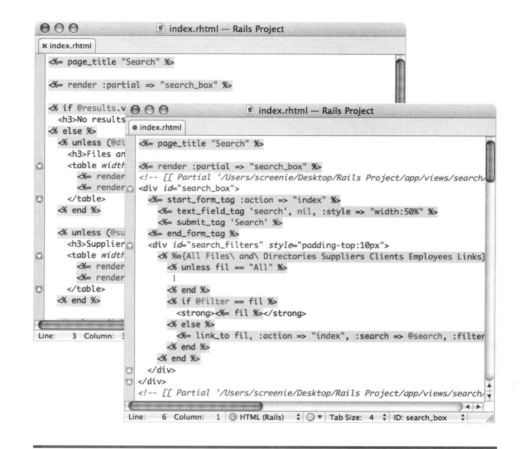

Figure 5.3: EDITING PARTIALS INLINE

As I said, you still need to handle the initial checkout before TextMate can help you with a repository. Luckily, that's just one command you need to feed the Terminal:

```
$ svn --username your.name.here checkout repository.url.here
```

After you have a checkout, just drag the top-level repository folder onto TextMate to create a project. This is a standard TextMate project just like the ones discussed in Chapter 2, *Projects*, on page 13. However, because this project is a Subversion checkout, you have access to the Subversion commands[2] for the files and directories contained within.

---

2.   If TextMate has trouble locating your installed copy of Subversion, you can guide it to the binary by setting the TM_SVN variable to the path of the executable. See Section 9.2, *TextMate's Environment Variables*, on page 113, for details on how to set environment variables inside TextMate.

Add to Repository	1
Remove From Repository...	2
Revert	3
Update to Newest (HEAD)	4
Commit...	**5**
Blame	6
Info	7
Log	8
View Revision...	9
Status for Selected Files	0
Diff Revisions...	
Diff With Newest (HEAD)	
Diff With Working Copy (BASE)	
Diff With Previous Revision (PREV)	
Diff With Revision...	
Diff Selected Files With Working Copy (BASE)	
Resolved	
Help	

Figure 5.4: SUBVERSION MENU

Let's examine where you can find those commands and what they will do for you. All the Subversion commands are mapped to the same keystroke, ^ ⇧ A, so that triggers a nice menu of choices. You can see what this menu looks like in Figure 5.4.

These commands work just as they do when interacting with Subversion in the Terminal, but you get to do everything from the comfort of TextMate. Commands that need input from you to operate will display GUI windows when invoked. For example, Commit will open a window that accepts your commit message and allows you to change the files included in the commit, and Diff with Revision will show a window that allows you to select the version to which to compare the current file. Many commands show their output using TextMate's HTML output window.

Commands that require file selections to work on use the files and directories selected in the project drawer. Therefore, if you want to update the entire project to the newest revision, make sure the top-level directory is selected in the project drawer.

Probably the biggest advantage of using the TextMate bundle over the shell is that the Diff commands pipe their results into a new TextMate document that will be syntax highlighted by the Diff bundle.[3] This makes it a lot easier to tell what is being added or removed.

Remember that the bundle isn't consulted when you use the project drawer to rename or delete some file. This can get you out of sync with the repository, which would add the missing files back with the next update. It's best not to use those features of TextMate when working with Subversion repositories.

5.6 The Math Bundle

Quick and dirty calculations are something we all do frequently. Sure, you can load Calculator, do the math, and bring back the results, but there's really no need for the context shift.

If you want to know the answer to a simple math question, such as how many seconds there are in a day, just ask TextMate. First, enter a formula:

```
60 * 60 * 24
```

Next, you can open the Math bundle's contextual menu with ^ ⇧ C (for "calculate"). Just as it was with Subversion, this is one-stop shopping for all things in the Math bundle. Now, the result you get depends on the command you choose. For example, picking Evaluate Line gives you the following:

```
60 * 60 * 24 = 86400
```

If you prefer to replace the calculation with the result, you could instead choose Evaluate and Replace Expression. If the calculation might use decimals and you prefer to have a whole-number result, use Evaluate and Replace Expression (Rounded).

The replacement versions are terrific for scaling some number inline without having to do any thinking. Just multiply or divide by the desired scale, select the formula, and let TextMate worry about the math.

So far you have been examining commands working on the current line. They will also work on a selection, if there is one, which allows you

---

3. You can also use the Diff bundle to compare local files, of course. Explore that bundle's menu for the commands that do this.

to evaluate subexpressions using the previous commands. Selections really shine with the middle three commands of the menu, though.

As an example, say you have a simple list of farm animals:

```
6 cows
2 sheep
1 Perl programmer
10 chickens
```

You don't have any math symbols here, but TextMate is not stymied by such trivialities. If you want to count the animals, by golly, you can!

If you select those lines in TextMate, call up the calculate menu, choose Add Numbers in Selection, and type a label for the new number, you get the following:

```
6 cows
2 sheep
1 Perl programmer
10 chickens = 19 farm animals
```

Notice how the command just found the numbers in the lines and didn't need any math operations to guide the process.

This is great for doing quick sums, and the sister command Subtract Numbers in Selection handles the opposite operation. Don't forget to try these commands on columnar selections, as described in Section 3.2, *Column Selections*, on page 26.

5.7 The Markdown Bundle

I mentioned earlier that the whole world is writing web pages now, but the great news is that you don't always need HTML to do it. A few higher-level languages simplify building at least some web page content. Markdown is one such language, focusing on a natural and readable syntax even before it's marked up.[4]

---

4.   You can find more details about Markdown at the official site: http://daringfireball.net/projects/markdown/.

Here's a trivial example of a Markdown document:

builtin_automations/example.markdown

```
Markdown Example
================

This is a simple paragraph containing markup for *italics* and **bold**.  It
also includes a couple of hyperlinks:  [The Pragmatic Programmers][pragprog] and
[TextMate][].

[pragprog]: http://www.pragmaticprogrammer.com/
[textmate]: http://macromates.com/

> We can insert quoted text just like this.

        or even include
          code, poetry, or
        anything else that is preformatted

Lists
-----

Markdown also supports lists, of course.  You can have unordered:

* application
* library
* framework

or ordered:

1. first
2. second
3. third

You can even nest:

1. Editing
        1.  Projects
        2.  Moving Around
        3.  Find and Replace
2. Automations
        1. Built-In Automations
        2. Snippets
        3. Macros
        4. Commands
```

This is easy syntax to get the hang of, but the bundle can still provide
plenty of help when you want to edit Markdown. If you don't know or
remember all the Markdown syntax, use the Syntax Cheat Sheet (⌃H in a
Markdown document) to brush up on it.

Now that you know the syntax and are ready to write, I'll point out some of my favorite shortcuts. First type your headers as usual, and then use Level 1 [setext] (= →|) and Level 2 [setext] (- →|) on the following line to underline the whole thing.

Another great help is that the bundle provides ⌘ I and ⌘ B for italics and bold, just like you would expect from a word processor. You can use those when you are ready to enter new content or with a selection to which to apply the markup.

Another big help is with lists. Inside any list item, just press ⌥ to create a new list item. For numbered lists, this will increase the count normally. You can also use ⇧ ⌥ to start a new sublist.

The Lookup Selection on Google and Link feature of the HTML bundle is also available in Markdown. To build a hyperlink off the first match in a Google search, select your link text, and trigger the command with ^ ⇧ ⌘ L. The link will be returned in Markdown syntax.

As you are working, remember that you can see the rendered HTML output anytime with the Preview command (^ ⌥ ⌘ P). If you are finished and want the end result in HTML form, you can use Convert Document to HTML (^ ⇧ H).

Here's the resulting output from the example at the beginning of this section (I also hit it with the Tidy command of the HTML bundle to make it look nice):

`builtin_automations/example.html`

```html
<!DOCTYPE html PUBLIC "-//W3C//DTD XHTML 1.0 Strict//EN"
    "http://www.w3.org/TR/xhtml1/DTD/xhtml1-strict.dtd">
<html xmlns="http://www.w3.org/1999/xhtml"><head>
    <title>Markdown to HTML</title>
</head><body>
    <h1 id="markdown_example">Markdown Example</h1>

    <p>
        This is a simple paragraph containing markup for <em>italics</em> and
        <strong>bold</strong>. It also includes a couple of hyperlinks:
        <a href="http://www.pragmaticprogrammer.com/">The Pragmatic Programmers</a>
        and <a href="http://macromates.com/">TextMate</a>.
    </p>

    <blockquote>
        <p>We can insert quoted text just like this.</p>
    </blockquote>
```

```
<pre>
    <code>or even include
            code, poetry, or
            anything else that is preformatted
    </code>
</pre>

<h2 id="lists">Lists</h2>

<p>Markdown also supports lists, of course. You can have unordered:</p>

<ul>
    <li>application</li>
    <li>library</li>
    <li>framework</li>
</ul>

<p>or ordered:</p>

<ol>
    <li>first</li>
    <li>second</li>
    <li>third</li>
</ol>

<p>You can even nest:</p>

<ol>
    <li>Editing
        <ol>
            <li>Projects</li>
            <li>Moving Around</li>
            <li>Find and Replace</li>
        </ol>
    </li>

    <li>Automations
        <ol>
            <li>Built-In Automations</li>
            <li>Snippets</li>
            <li>Macros</li>
            <li>Commands</li>
        </ol>
    </li>
</ol>
</body></html>
```

If you're a fan of the enhanced MultiMarkdown syntax, you will find that all the automations I just discussed work there too; in addition, the extra output options are available in the MultiMarkdown submenu of this bundle. If you prefer a more developer-centric language such as Textile, you'll be happy to hear that there is a bundle for that too, and several of the shortcuts described earlier work the same in that syntax.

5.8 The Blogging Bundle

Once you get hooked on TextMate automations, it will be hard to convince yourself to edit text in anything else. Luckily, you seldom need to do so. Blogging is a great example. If your blog supports the meta-Weblog API like Movable Type (MT), WordPress, and Typo do, odds are TextMate can talk to it. I'll show you how to give it a shot.

First, you need to tell TextMate where to find your blog. Don't worry, that's not hard at all. Just choose Bundles → Blogging → Setup Blogs. It will open the configuration file the bundle commands use to do their work. You need to place a line in this file depending on your type of blog. For example:

```
MT Blog Name           http://username@domain.com/mt/mt-xmlrpc.cgi#1
WordPress Blog Name    http://username@domain.com/blog/xmlrpc.php
Typo Blog Name         http://username@domain.com/backend/xmlrpc
```

Then, after adding the right URL, you should be able to test the connection. To do so, choose Bundles → Blogging → Fetch Post. You will be prompted for a password if this is your first connection attempt, but the bundle will remember it for future access. If you get a dialog box containing a menu of recent posts, you're all set. Select one to open so you can see what they look like. Note the headers up top and the post content below that.

Now you are free to edit the post you just opened and activate Post to Blog (^ ⌘ P) to update it on your host. More often, though, you'll probably want to create new posts. To do that, create a new blog post from one of the provided templates. You can find those under File → New From Template → Blogging. Just select the format your blog is set to receive posts in: Markdown, Textile, HTML, or plain text.

In the new document you will see a place to give your post a title. You may want to add other headers for this post as well; the Blogging bundle has snippets and commands for this in the Headers submenu. The one I often add to a new post is Category (cat ↹) so the post will appear in the correct blog category. It can fetch a category list from your blog and will give you a dialog box of choices for the post. You can add this header multiple times, specifying a new category each time, to place the post in multiple locations. The Category dialog box will do this for you, if you make multiple selections by ⌘-clicking the names.

When your headers are set, it's time to create the blog post body. You can create a summary for your post above that funny divider line in the template and place extended content below the divider, or you can remove the divider altogether and type the full post to be used both on the post page and in post listings. Remember that you have access to all the TextMate automations for the language type you selected, so don't forget to use all those great shortcuts!

If you want images in the post, just drag them onto your document at the correct insertion point. The image will be uploaded to your blog, and a URL will be dropped into the document to reference it. If you want to rename the image on upload, hold down the ⌥ key during the drag.

As usual for TextMate, you can preview your post with the Preview command (^ ⌥ ⌘ P). When you have things as you want them, uploading is as simple as triggering Post to Blog (^ ⌘ P). This action will update the post document with all the header information of the post. You can edit this document and repost, if you notice any errors.

5.9 The Mail Bundle

If you edit your blog posts in TextMate, it's only a short step to wanting to edit your email in the same place. This is probably overkill for a quick one-line response message, but when you are editing bigger messages, it's nice to have access to all of TextMate's editing tools and automations. You will still need a mail client to handle the retrievals and send messages, but if you installed Edit in TextMate as I suggested in Section 1.4, *Installing TextMate and Tools*, on page 6, you're only one keystroke away from doing the actual editing in your favorite editor. This requires a Cocoa mail client, such as Apple's Mail.

When you want to edit a message in TextMate, just place your caret in the message body, and then trigger Edit → Edit in TextMate (^ ⌘ E). Your message will be moved to the editor where you can add whatever you like. When you're done, just save the message, and it will be updated in the email client application from which it was pulled.

If your message comes from Apple's Mail program, TextMate should assign the proper syntax. If you use a different program, just select Mail from the language menu at the bottom of the editing window. The Mail

---

Hidden Commands

Not all commands are in the menus. The Text bundle has a nice command attached to ⌥ that you can trigger inside any URL to open it in your web browser. The Source bundle has its own command on ⌥ that will continue a line comment in source code on the next line.

These commands don't make much sense except when triggered with a keyboard shortcut, so they don't have menu presences. I'll show you how to find hidden commands in Section 9.1, *Building Bundle Menus*, on page 111.

---

syntax is an extension of the Markdown syntax, so you can use everything I described in Section 5.7, *The Markdown Bundle*, on page 67, in addition to the commands I am about to cover.

This bundle has only a handful of shortcuts, but they can be a real boon when cleaning up email messages. First, know that you can use ⌘' and ⌥⌘' to increase or decrease the current quote level just as you can in Apple's own Mail program.

The other big wins here are the Reformat Quoted Text (^Q) and Unwrap Paragraphs (^⇧Q) commands. With the former you can rewrap lines beginning with one or more levels of email quoting. With the latter you can strip hard line breaks from message content. Both problems should be familiar to anyone who has spent time manually correcting emails.

5.10 The Text Bundle

TextMate also includes a bundle for general text transformation that can be useful no matter what kind of document you are editing. I'll tell you about two automations I use from that bundle all the time.

First, when you are writing up your five-star review of this book for Slashdot,[5] be sure to remember that Slashdot likes a minimum of 800 words. Instead of counting those by hand, I recommend using the Statistics for Document (Word Count) command of the Text bundle. You can trigger that at any time with ^⇧N, and when you do, TextMate will open

---

5. http://slashdot.org/

Figure 5.5: WORD COUNT TOOLTIP

a tooltip with line, word, and byte (characters for ASCII documents) counts. For an example of what this looks like, see Figure 5.5.

Another not-to-miss feature of the Text bundle is the handy Lorem ipsum snippet for generating instant content. It's common to know that you will need some text in a document but not yet know what that text might be. You can generate placeholder text in TextMate by typing lorem→ι, which will conjure up the following:

```
Lorem ipsum dolor sit amet, consectetur adipisicing elit, sed do eiusmod
tempor incididunt ut labore et dolore magna aliqua. Ut enim ad minim
veniam, quis nostrud exercitation ullamco laboris nisi ut aliquip ex ea
commodo consequat. Duis aute irure dolor in reprehenderit in voluptate
velit esse cillum dolore eu fugiat nulla pariatur. Excepteur sint
occaecat cupidatat non proident, sunt in culpa qui officia deserunt
mollit anim id est laborum.
```

The previous text is a tool of the publishing and graphical design industries that is used to shift focus away from content and to the presentation. It approximates a typical character distribution for English and thus makes natural placeholder content.

That's not all there is to the Text bundle; I encourage you to go poking around in there for more goodies. I regularly use Remove Unprintable Characters in Document, Delete Line, and Duplicate Line, which all do what their names imply. There are also handy snippets for inserting a copyright notice or the current date.

5.11 The Source Bundle

Another general bundle included with TextMate holds automations for manipulating source code. If you use TextMate for programming, you will definitely want to commit at least two of these helpers to memory.

If you've worked with code for any amount of time, you have experienced the need to comment and uncomment sections of code. It's a pretty fundamental need of programming. The Comment Line/Selection command of this bundle, available in any language via ⌘/, handles both sides of the process. Select the text to comment or uncomment, and trigger the command to toggle the presence of comment markers based on the current language.

Another shortcut of this bundle deals directly with an oddity of working with all this automation. During automation-assisted editing, it's quite common to finish creating a line of code but have your caret still be in the middle of that line. When that happens, you can use the Move to EOL automations to skip ahead. My favorite is bound to ⌘↩, which will hop to the end of the line and press ↩ for you (to create a new line). If you are using a language requiring a line terminator, such as the common semicolon, use ⇧⌘↩ instead, and TextMate will insert the terminator before pressing ↩.

Play around a bit with the other shortcuts in this bundle to see whether any catch your eye. I find Toggle Single/Double Quotes (^ ") and everything in the Insert Escaped submenu to be pretty handy when dealing with programming language strings.

5.12   The TextMate Bundle

TextMate also includes a set of automations useful for interacting with the application itself. I will introduce some of these later when they are helpful to what I am discussing at the time, but a few of these commands are too useful to wait.

Sharing documents over the internet without losing formatting is a problem most of us have faced. You can't really copy and paste significant content into an instant message, email message, or IRC client with much success because often limits exist on message size and the formatting is generally lost. A solution for this that has recently become popular is to use a pasting service and then just send the link for the document to the intended recipient. TextMate will do this for you.

To try this, open any document you have been working on, select a portion of it you don't mind sharing publicly on the internet, and activate the Paste Selection Online command (^ ⌥ ⇧ V). TextMate will present you with a dialog box that allows you to select where to send the link to the document. You are free to make multiple selections while holding down the ⌘ key. Since you are just testing this here, choose Open in Browser.

You should be taken to your document's location on the pasting service. Take a look around, because a lot of benefit is packed into that one little command. If you were working with a document type TextMate recognized, your paste should retain its syntax highlighting. Viewers of the paste can even use the menu to select a TextMate theme in order to color the document. Your lines will be numbered as well, and, of course, there is a link to download the content.

Taking a step back, you have other options for where you can send pastes. The dialog box should include any IRC channels you are currently in if you use Colloquy[6] as your client. You should also be able to send the link to any of your instant messaging contacts if you use iChat or Adium[7] for a client. If none of that works for you, though, just choose Send to Clipboard, then paste the link wherever you need it.

Now, if you need to place document content in a web page of your own, you will want to get to know the Create HTML from Document, Create HTML from Document with Line Numbers, and Create CSS from Current Theme commands. They function exactly as advertised by their names, "HTM-Lifying" your document content into an instant web page. Try these commands too so you can see for yourself: Open any document that TextMate will syntax highlight, select Create HTML from Document with Line Numbers, and, after the new web page source pops up, see how it looks with TextMate's built-in Show Web Preview (^ ⌥ ⌘ P).

As you can see, TextMate has tools for your specific focus, no matter what it is. The truth is that I haven't covered even a fourth of what is available in this chapter, but you should now be more equipped to explore the bundles of interest to you. Sooner or later, though, you will realize that you can take all this wonderful automation to the next level if you can fine-tune it to your unique needs. You're now ready to see how to do exactly that.

---

6. http://colloquy.info/
7. http://adiumx.com/

Chapter 6

Snippets

Snippets are the simplest form of automation in TextMate. They're kind of like having a high-tech version of my grandmother available to you at all times. You see, whenever I mention an interest to my grandmother or tell her about something I did, it triggers her Snippet Reflex (patent pending). From that point on whenever she reads anything related in the newspaper, in a magazine, or off the back of a grocery bag, she clips the item and mails it to me.

With my grandmother, the mention of an interest is a trigger, and the resulting action is getting an article about it. This simple association of a trigger and a response is exactly what TextMate's snippets are. That's right, every copy of TextMate ships with my poor grandmother bundled up inside, and if you mention something to her, she will mail the complete article right into your document post-haste. Luckily, it doesn't take longer to build most snippets than it does to mention things to my grandmother, so the savings in your work can be quite significant.

6.1 Basic Snippets

Enough talk, let's build some snippets! First, you need to create a bundle called Pragmatic Examples. See Chapter 5, *Built-in Automations*, on page 53, for a definition of what a TextMate bundle is. You'll use this new bundle as your workspace. It will hold the examples you will play with in these next few chapters plus any extra experiments you want to try on your own. You can later refer to this bundle to remember the tricks you've learned, or you can easily toss it out when you don't need it anymore.

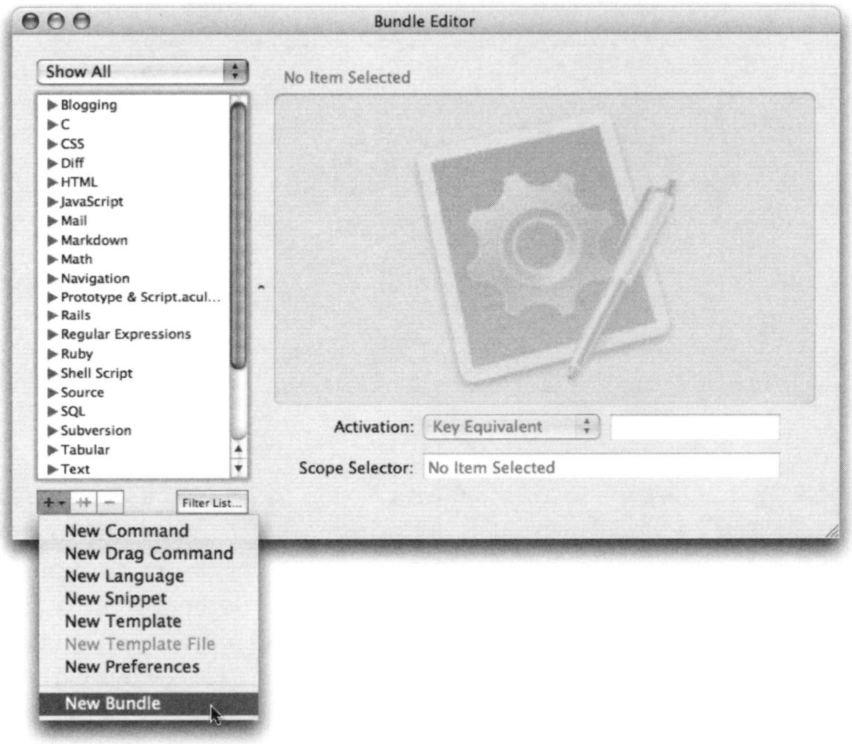

Figure 6.1: CREATING A NEW BUNDLE

Here's how to create your own bundle:

1. Open the Bundle Editor by choosing Bundles → BundleEditor → Show Bundle Editor (^ ⌥ ⌘ B).

2. Open the + menu in the lower-left corner of the Bundle Editor, and choose New Bundle.

3. Give your test bundle the name Pragmatic Examples.

Let's start with a trivial snippet that saves me time every day. I'm in the habit of using my full name on pretty much everything, because my name is just a little too common. Now, I don't want to type James Edward Gray II all the time. It's too long, and I know I would make errors. That's why I have a snippet for my name, which you can see in Figure 6.2, on the next page. In this snippet, the trigger is typing in my initials followed by a tab, and the action is that my entire name appears in the document. It's my grandmother all over again.

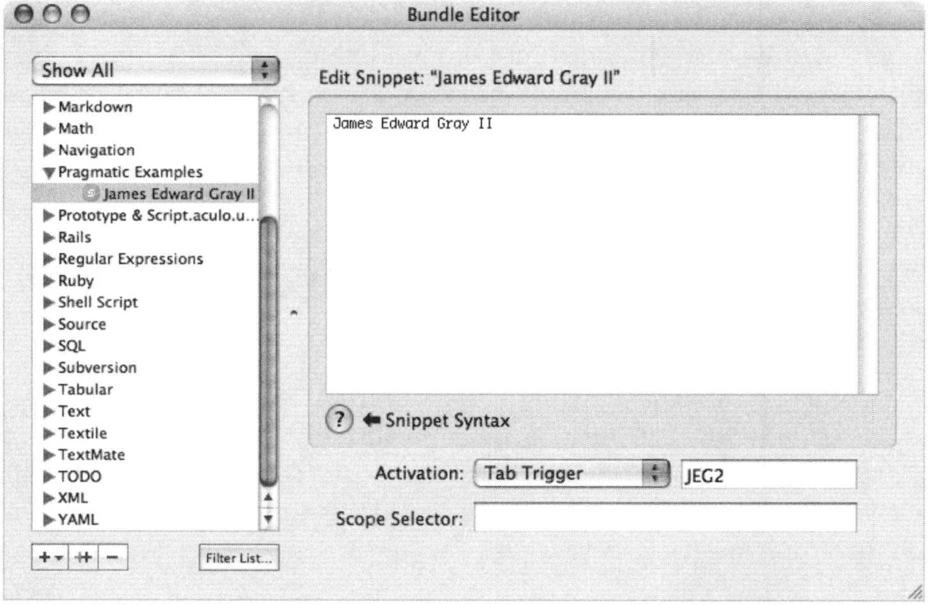

Figure 6.2: MY NAME SNIPPET

Create a new snippet inside the Pragmatic Examples bundle. While you are still in the Bundle Editor, try this:

1. Highlight your new bundle on the left side of the Bundle Editor. Clicking the name Pragmatic Examples will do that.
2. Open the + menu in the lower-left corner of the Bundle Editor, and choose New Snippet.
3. Type your full name as the name for this snippet.

You now have a blank snippet to use. Well, it's not completely blank. Check out the cheat sheet that comes with the snippet-in-the-making. It's a reminder of all the special syntax you can use in your new snippet.

Go ahead and replace the cheat sheet text with your full name, which will be inserted when you trigger the snippet. Then set Activation to Tab Trigger, and put your initials in that field. Close the Bundle Editor so TextMate will save your work, and play with your new snippet by entering your initials into a document and pressing ⇥. *Tab triggers* are always used this way. You type the trigger and then press ⇥. The full word to the left of the caret will then be replaced with the contents of the snippet.

There is not much to this shortcut, but I can type JEG2→ in any document and have it expanded into my full name. That saves me fifteen keystrokes every time I type my name and prevents 100 percent of the typos I used to make when typing it in full. If I misspell the trigger, it is obvious to me when it doesn't expand, and I then just correct it.

Many TextMate users would probably set the tab trigger to "James"—that would be fine too. The thinking there is that you can just start typing what you want and then expand it into the complete piece of text. This is often a great idea and is a natural way to work.

Sometimes, though, I use a mnemonic trigger instead, like "JEG2"—I use that as a shortcut for my name all the time, so it is easy for me to remember. Also, if I use my standard shortcut somewhere and then decide I want to switch it to my full name, it's just one keystroke to change my mind.

Either way, you will generally want to use tab triggers for snippets. *Key equivalents* require more effort to remember and thus are better suited for actions you want TextMate to take instead of bits of text to insert. Tab triggers, on the other hand, flow naturally from document content, making them ideal for most insertions.

Before I show you any fancy snippet tricks, I'll add one final point about plain-text insertion: The replacement text doesn't always have to be longer than the trigger. For example, I also have the inverse snippet that truncates my full name down to the initials. I don't use that as often as the first snippet, but it still comes in handy.

6.2 Tab Stops

It's common in many text-editing tasks to want to enter several pieces of different information all in the same skeleton format. For example, the header of a web page (just an HTML text file) often looks similar among all the pages of the site, but you might need to tweak the title of each page in that header.[1] In TextMate, you handle these variations with *tab stop* variables.

Let's say you want to keep a simple text file of contact information. Perhaps your company is not yet big enough to warrant the cost and training time for a contact management software package, and the text

---

1. There is a snippet in the default HTML bundle for this: Head.

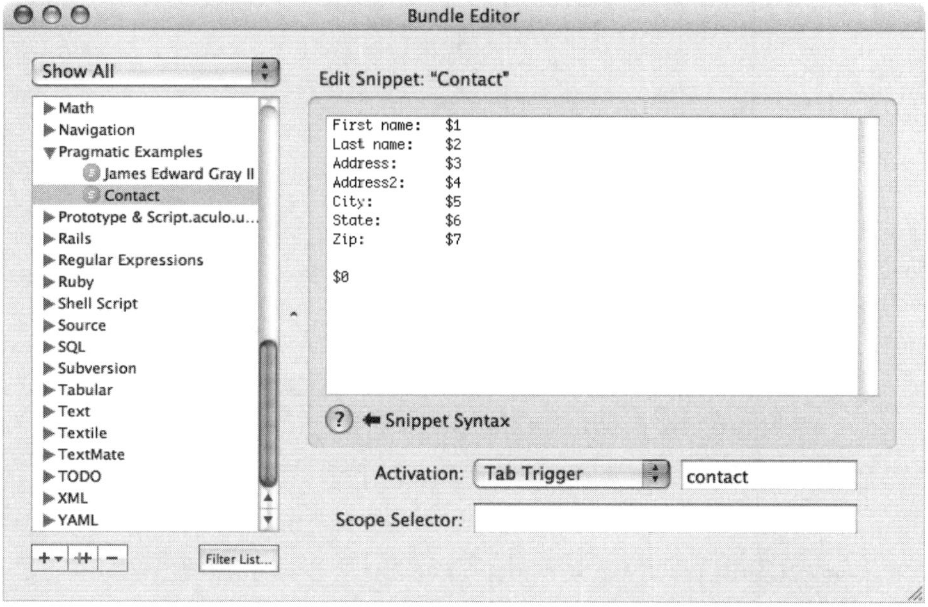

Figure 6.3: A CONTACT INFORMATION SNIPPET

format combined with some trivial scripts give you all the flexibility you need. See Figure 6.3 for a snippet you might use in this case.

The new element here is the addition of the funny-looking $1 style variables. You can use these variables to help TextMate hop the caret around a snippet as if it were a form, allowing the user to fill in the blanks. You still get the inserted text, but now you can move the caret from tab stop to tab stop (using the →| key, of course) in the order of the variable numbers. You can even go backward in the form to correct mistakes (using |←). See Figure 6.4, on the next page, for an example of how this plays out in usage.

Before I move on to the next feature of snippets, I'll talk a little more about where they end. Do you notice that $0 tab stop at the end of the previous example? It's a little different from the other tab stops. First, it is always the last tab stop in the list. If you defined $1, $2, and $3 in a snippet, then $0 would be tabbed to after $3. The other special quirk about $0 is that the snippet form magic ends as soon as you tab to it.

Reaching the end of a snippet has two effects. First, you can no longer →| or |← between the fields, which is the downside. The upside is that you do regain access to tab triggers for activating other snippets. For

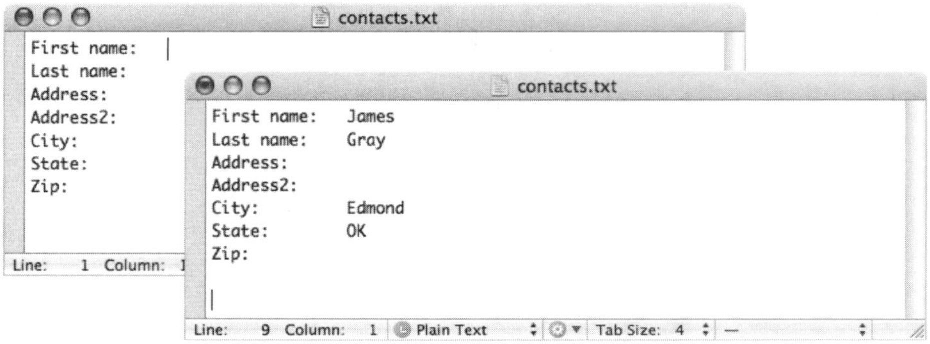

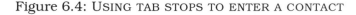

Figure 6.4: USING TAB STOPS TO ENTER A CONTACT

that reason, you often want to set $0 as the tab stop for the main content portion of a snippet so you can use other snippets when you get there. Don't worry if your placement of $0 leaves the caret in the middle of a line or document. The user can always jump the caret around easily enough with the techniques described in Section 3.1, *Moving Around*, on page 21.

If you do not include a $0 variable and the last thing in your snippet is not a tab stop, TextMate adds an implicit $0 to the tail end of the snippet upon insertion. Even if you have a tab stop followed by whitespace (including a newline character) at the end, TextMate will add a $0. If the last thing in your snippet is a tab stop variable, it assumes the $0 snippet-ending behavior.

Placeholders

If you refer to Figure 6.4, you will see that with the contact snippet I knew what to enter at each point, because of the labels at the beginning of each line. At times, though, what to enter may not be so obvious. Also, sometimes what you enter doesn't change too often and you'd like a reasonable default with the option to change it as needed. TextMate has an answer for both of these instances; it's called *placeholders*.

Placeholders are default text inserted at that tab stop. After the snippet is triggered and the user tabs to that stop, the default text is selected. From there the user can move on to the next field or start typing to replace the default with the needed text. This also allows you to give names to tab stops to remind users what belongs in that space.

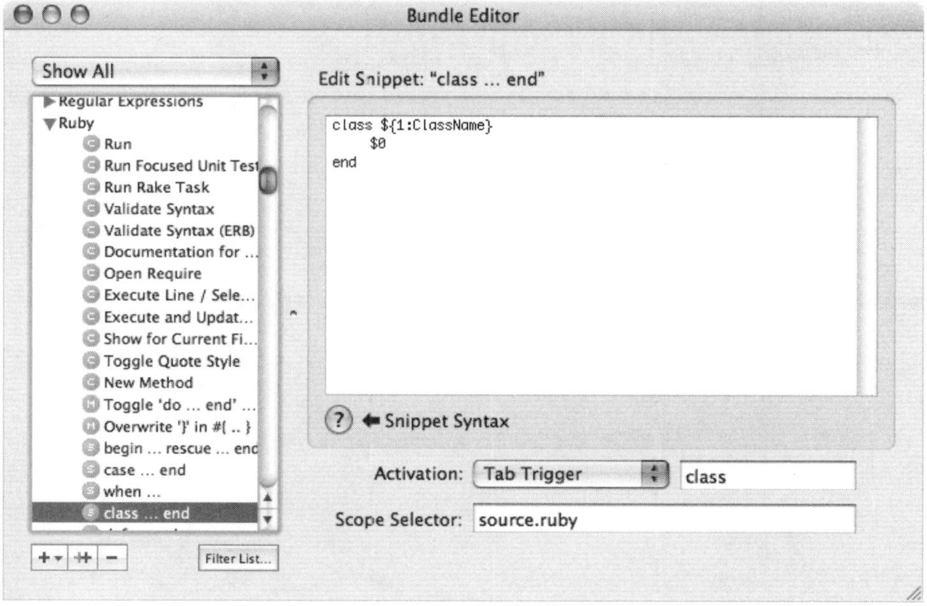

Figure 6.5: The Ruby bundle class snippet

See Figure 6.5 for an example of a placeholder snippet from the Ruby bundle that comes with TextMate. You can trigger that snippet by making sure you are in a Ruby document and entering class⇥. When it appears, the ClassName default text will be selected, as shown in Figure 6.6, on the next page. Pressing ⇥ again tells TextMate you are fine with the default and skips you into the next tab stop to create the class body. In this case, though, the default isn't useful since you are probably trying to build a unique Ruby class. The text does provide you with a nice reminder of what you should enter there, though, including the CamelCase-style convention for Ruby class names.

This snippet is also a good example of the special $0 variable in action. A class body can be large and involved, so you want the user to have access to all the Ruby snippets when coding it. That's why I used $0 here. You can tab to it, and then the snippet ends.

Let's dig into one more snippet of the Ruby bundle for another great placeholder trick. Specifically, you need to know that placeholders can be nested, like this:

```
:${1:key} => ${2:"S{3:value}"}${4:, }
```

Figure 6.6: THE CLASSNAME PLACEHOLDER

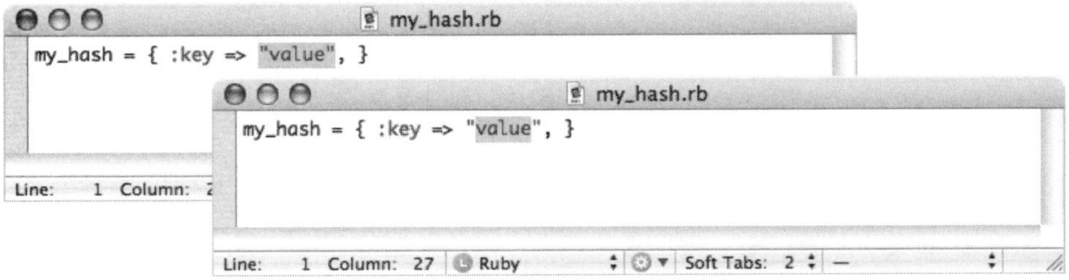

Figure 6.7: USING NESTED TAB STOPS

When building a Ruby Hash, it's common to use a quoted string as the second half of a pair. Of course, it is about equally common to use a variable, which would not need the quotes. This snippet can handle either case. When you reach the second tab stop, the quotes and content will be selected, and you can type in a variable name or any Ruby expression. However, if you do want a quoted string, tab one more time to select just the content inside the quotes and replace that instead. (See Figure 6.7.) It's important to note here that you could reverse the order if you prefer. If the $2 variable held the inner content and the $3 variable held that plus the quotes, you would reach the inner string first and could ⇥ to expand the selection to include the quotes.

Mirroring and Transformations

Being able to use the tab stop variables is certainly helpful and adding placeholders for defaults or reminders are even better, but TextMate takes the variable trick one step further.

Working with text formats can be repetitive. You often need to place some piece of text in multiple places, and you can do that in your snippets with *mirroring*.

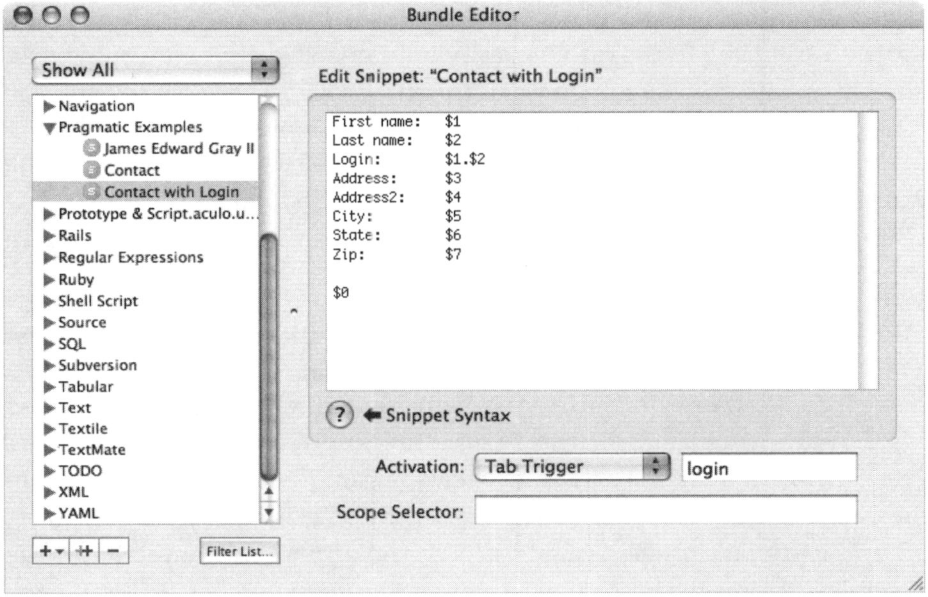

Figure 6.8: A CONTACT SNIPPET WITH LOGIN GENERATION

Referring to the earlier contact snippet example, let's say you also want to generate a login for your website for each contact you work with. This is a job for mirroring, and you can see it in action in Figure 6.8, where a login is generated by combining the contact's first and last names around a period.

Notice how the variables $1 and $2 are in there twice now? The first time they appear is where the entry will actually take place. All other occurrences are mirrors. They will duplicate the contents of what is entered at the first occurrence, as you type even. Isn't that cool?

Now what would be even better is if you could modify the generated login to be a bit shorter and not require the user to type capital letters. Oh, and you can! TextMate calls that a *transformation*, which is a mirror with minor adjustments. Transformations, like much of TextMate, are powered by the regular expression engine. If you can remember all the way back to Section 4.2, *Mixing in Regular Expressions*, on page 42, you're all set. To generate easier-to-type logins, just change the login line of the last snippet to this:

```
Login:        ${1/^.*?(\w).*$/\L$1/}.${2/^.*?(\S+).*$/\L$1/}
```

This time I am transforming the variables before they are duplicated. You can see that the variable syntax changes slightly, allowing you to place a regular expression between the first two forward slashes and the replacement expression between the last two. In other words, transformations always have the form ${#/expression/replacement/} where # is the variable you want to change, expression is the regular expression used to find the content you want to change, and replacement is the text with which to replace the match.

In the login example, the transformation for the $1 isolates the first word character from whatever is before and after it and then replaces the entire contents of the variable with just that character, in lowercase. The replacement for the $2 variable is similar, but it locates the first run of nonwhitespace characters (a word) and uses just that in the replacement, again in lowercase. That will ensure I just get *gray* if I enter my last name as *Gray II*. The replacements are made on the variables before they are displayed.

If you are using simple mirrors, the first occurrence of the variable is the actual placement. However, the variable can be preceded by transforms that will be skipped over when the user tabs. For an example of how this might be useful, see Figure 6.9, on the next page, where a proper ID is set for the HTML header tag based on the header typed.

The /g modifier at the end of that transform performs a "global" search and replace. When you add that option, the change will be made in every place the expression matches instead of just in the first match. This is a common modifier for transform operations.

If you want a regular mirror but would rather the tab stop be to a later variable, give the later variable some default text or use a regular expression on the first variable that replaces nothing, like this: ${1/\A(?!)//}. Remember that the mirroring and transformation magic stops along with the tab stop functionality as soon as the user reaches the final tab stop (usually $0).

Getting Snippet Data from TextMate and the Shell

The following two features aren't used as commonly, but you may still find uses for them from time to time. First, TextMate maintains several variables that are available inside snippets (and other automations). Probably the most common one to use in snippets is $TM_SELECTED_TEXT. That variable holds the current selection, when there is one.

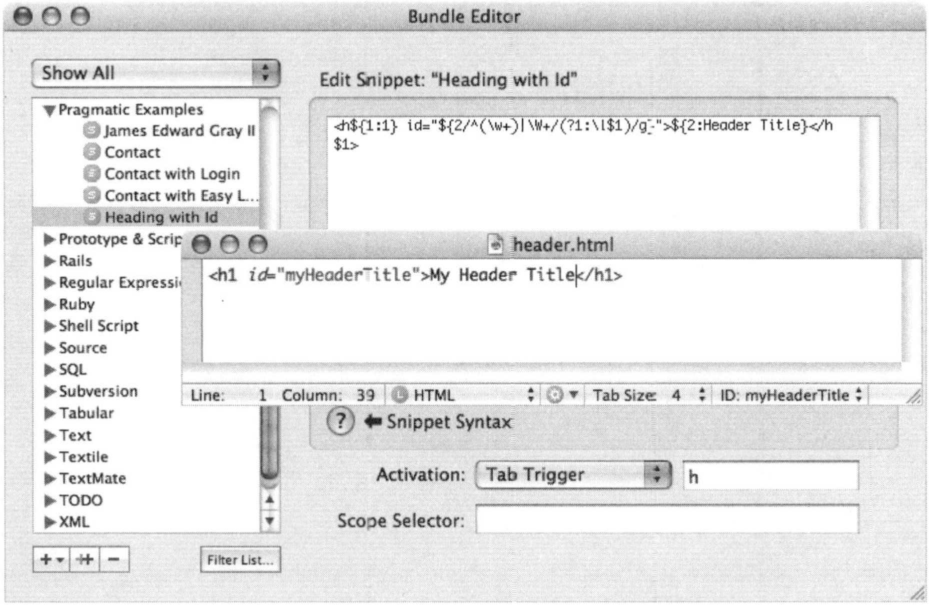

Figure 6.9: AN HTML HEADER SNIPPET WITH ID GENERATION

I said earlier that most snippets should use tab triggers, and when you activate a tab trigger, it's impossible for there to be a selection (because you just typed the trigger and pressed ⇥). $TM_SELECTED_TEXT won't help you there. However, that's only one way to activate a snippet. You can always select a snippet from the Bundles menu, even if it has a tab trigger assigned. You might also decide this is a special snippet that deserves a key equivalent instead of a tab trigger. In either case, there could be a selection, and when there is, you can use $TM_SELECTED_TEXT to get it.

Let's build a pretty curly quotes example for HTML. You will bind it to a key equivalent of ^" and allow it to be activated from the menu with a selection you would like to quote. You can see the snippet in Figure 6.10, on the following page.

As you can see, I just used the variable contents as the default placeholder. When there's no selection, the content will be empty, and the user can type what they want. If there was a selection, though, the quote entities will be added around it.

See Section 9.2, *TextMate's Environment Variables*, on page 113, for a complete list of the TextMate variables.

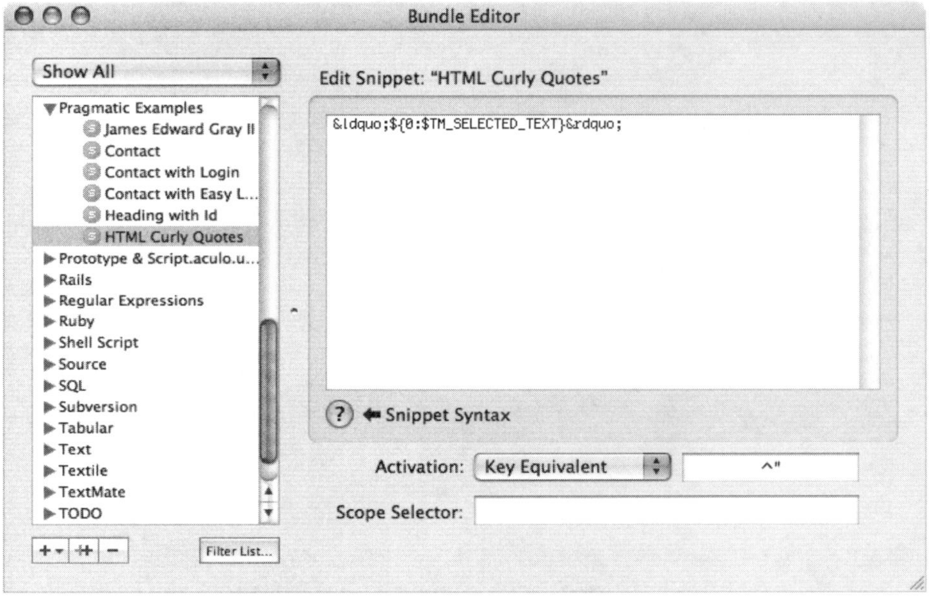

Figure 6.10: A CURLY QUOTES SNIPPET FOR HTML

One last way to get data for a snippet is to *shell out* for it. You can make calls to any Unix shell commands inside a snippet, dumping the results into the output. Probably the most common use for this is to fetch the current date or time using the date command. For example, adding `date +%Y-%m-%d` in a snippet will fetch a date similar in form to 2006-06-04. You can shell out to any Unix command you like. See Section 9.3, *Useful Shell Commands*, on page 118 for a list of oft-used commands.

Limiting Snippet Scope

I have been playing fast and loose with the Scope Selector field so far, yet all the snippets have just worked. If you don't specify a *scope*, Text-Mate makes the snippet available globally. Sometimes, that's handy. I want to be able to use my name snippet everywhere, for example. However, there are also good reasons to limit the scope. I'll talk a little about those now.

There are two great reasons to limit scope. First, you have only so many keys on your keyboard. Although you can use the modifier keys to generate quite a few combinations, you eventually run out of good keys.

```
● ● ●                          📄 scope.xml
  <gedcom>
    <indi Id='@I1l@'>
      <name>Ith text.xml
          <surn meta.tag.xml
          <givn string.quoted.single.xml
      </name>
      <sex>F</sex>
      <_uid>38CC16658231D511ACB8E07C9CE21378E1AF</_uid>
      <fams>@F12@</fams>
      <famc>@F4@</famc>
    </indi>
  </gedcom>

Line:   2  Column:  18  🕐 XML          ↕ 🔘 ▼  Tab Size:  4  ↕ —                    ↕
```

Figure 6.11: EXAMINING TEXTMATE'S SCOPE

The other reason is related but still unique. In short, just because you use some tab trigger or key equivalent for one kind of document doesn't mean you don't want to use it in another kind of document. Wouldn't it be nice to be able to make TextMate recognize which context you are currently in and take the most appropriate action based on that, even if several automations share the same activation? That's exactly why you use TextMate's Scope Selector.

Now the first thing you need is the ability to find out what scope you are currently in. This helps you decide what to limit a snippet to. The TextMate bundle includes a command for this called simply Show Scope (^ ⇧ P). Try opening some document format TextMate recognizes, hopping the caret around to elements colored differently by the syntax highlighting[2] and activating the Show Scope command. You will see tooltips describing the hierarchy, like the one in Figure 6.11.

Selecting a scope for the snippet to be active in is as easy as you might guess. You limit the snippet to working inside strings with string or inside Ruby code with source.ruby. When TextMate resolves them, the more specific target beats a less specific one. So, a string.quoted snippet will be chosen over a string snippet with the same activation, assuming you are in the scope text.xml meta.tag.xml string.quoted.double.xml. Notice also that you need to give a prefix of only the actual scope you would like to match. All scopes starting with what you specify will have the snippet available.

---

2. Scopes are used for this too, and I'll discuss that more in Chapter 11, *Preferences and Themes*, on page 171.

You aren't limited to a single scope specifier either. Try using source.ruby string to match string scopes but only those inside Ruby source code files. You can be as specific as you need. If you need to support multiple scopes, just separate them with a comma: string, comment. Even more fun, you can subtract scopes. For example, let's say you have a snippet you would like to be available only in the content or nontag portions of an XML document. You can target that by targeting the XML scope and subtracting out the tag scope: text.xml - meta.tag.xml.

Snippets can take the sting out of repetitive data entry, and they take only moments to set up. That makes them well worth the effort to learn. When you're ready to shave repetitive editing steps off your workload, though, you will need a new tool. I'll talk about that next.

Chapter 7

Macros

Editing text documents is often repetitive work. We all eventually run into a task that requires the same series of steps to be done over and over again. In TextMate, you can build macros for this.

TextMate's macro engine is like a high-powered, text-editing video recorder. You can just press Record, do some editing, and then hit Stop. Once you have a macro recorded, you can rewind and play it again to repeat the edits as needed. So far your macro is only in temporary memory. If you create another macro, you will lose the first one. If the macro could be useful to you in the long-term, you are welcome to pull the video out of the machine and label it so you can find it again whenever you need it.

Let's build a macro so you can see one in action. Follow along with me as I build this one:

1. Create an empty TextMate document by choosing File → New (⌘ N).
2. Type a number into the document so you have some content to use. I used 9999.
3. Turn on macro recording with Bundles → Macros → Start Recording (⌥ ⌘ M). A red recording light should begin flashing in the lower-right corner of the editing window.
4. Take a deep breath and relax. I know this seems like a silly step, but I always feel like I'm under pressure when I start recording a macro. You're not. There's no time limit, and TextMate will patiently wait on you to think through how to proceed. It will remove any pauses you make when it replays the macro. Take your time.

5. Select the current word with ^W, and move to the end of that word by tapping →. You were probably already at the end of the number, but using this trick to find the end makes your macro work even when the caret is in the middle of a number.

6. Type a + followed by a 1.

7. Now you need to select the math expression you created. Hold down ⇧ so you can select as you move the caret, and tap ← twice. The first tap should select the 1, and the second will grab the +. Now you need the entire number that was there to begin with; you can select that by holding down ⇧ to select, holding down ⌥ to move word by word, and tapping ← one last time. You should now have the whole expression selected.

8. Let's do some math, TextMate style. Hit ^⇧C to open the calculation menu, and choose Evaluate and Replace Expression (you can just press 2 for this).

9. To finish, tap → to jump back to the end of our number.

10. Choose Bundles → Macros → Stop Recording (⌥⌘M). The red recording light should stop flashing.

You are now armed with a macro. Try running it a few more times on your number by choosing Bundles → Macros → Replay Last Recording (⇧⌘M). Place your caret in different places inside the number as you do this. Your number should climb each time the macro is triggered.

Currently the macro is just a scratch macro. You have access to it because it is the last one you recorded, but you would lose it if you recorded another one. You can use this process to repeat some content-specific operations a few times without worrying about the need to save the macro. If the macro is generally useful, though, you will want to keep it. Here's how to save what you just created:

1. Choose Bundles → Macros → Save Last Recording (^⌘M).

2. Type a meaningful name for your macro such as Increment Number.

3. Give the macro a key equivalent if you like. I used ^+.

4. If TextMate didn't add the macro to your Pragmatic Examples bundle, click the macro's name in the listing on the left side of the Bundle Editor, drag it onto the bundle you want to save it in, and drop it.

With your macro saved, you should be able to jump into your budget files, click random numbers, and bang on your assigned key equivalent to rapidly increase the amounts of cash you are spending and receiving.

That simple macro used native TextMate functions for selecting and moving, typing new content, and using a command from the Math bundle. I even used keyboard shortcuts to trigger them. As you can see, you can record most tasks you do when editing documents by using TextMate's macros. Exceptions exist, though.

If you triggered a command that requested input via a dialog box, TextMate would have no way to know what you fed the script and thus would not be able to re-create the result. TextMate also does not track changes you make in the project drawer, such as renaming files, and it has no way to track what you do in external programs. Most regular editing tasks work fine, though.

The rule of thumb is that changes that happen in the editing window are recorded. Typing and deleting clearly change the content of the editing window, so they work fine. Moving the caret around or making a selection is at least changing the caret in the editing window, so that counts. You can use Find and Replace commands and most automations, whether they ship with TextMate or you created them.

Let's look at one more example macro and one more feature that macros can take advantage of. Here are the steps to create a Fetch Web Page Source macro similar to the View Source command in most browsers:

1. Create an empty TextMate document (⌘N).
2. Type a web page URL into the document, but omit the "http://" protocol identifier. I used the URL of the Ruby Quiz site I run, rubyquiz.com.
3. Begin recording a macro (⌥⌘M).
4. Select the URL line by using ⌘→ to move to the end of the line and then pressing ⇧⌘← to drag a selection to the beginning of the line.
5. Now you need to fix the URL. Open the Find dialog box (⌘F). Enter the Find pattern as ^(? http://) and the Replace pattern as http://, and make sure Regular Expression is checked. Make the replacement in the current selection with ^⇧⌘F. Press ⌘W to dismiss the Find dialog box. This will add the protocol, if the link doesn't already have one.
6. The URL is fixed, so let's take it from a harmless little address to a full-fledged command. Press ⌘X to cut the link and place it on the clipboard, type require "open-uri"; open(", paste the URL back with ⌘V, and finish off the command by typing ") { |page| page.read }.

7. Let's ask TextMate to run our mini-Ruby program now and drop the results right into the editing window. Choose Bundles → Ruby → Execute Line as Ruby (^ ⇧ E). You need to have an active Internet connection for this step, and it may take a moment to run. You will know it is finished when the source of the web page appears below the command.

8. You should remove your scratch work, so you need to get the caret back there. Press ⌘ ↑ to return to the beginning of the document, open the Find dialog box with ⌘ F, enter a Find pattern of ^require "open-uri";, and press ↵ to hunt down the command. Select Bundles → Text → Delete Line (^ ⇧ K).

9. Stop macro recording (⌥ ⌘ M).

When you save this macro in the Bundle Editor, note that the Use Local Clipboard While Executing Macro checkbox is selected. You place the URL on the clipboard at one point during the macro's execution. If this option were deactivated, running the macro could surprise the user by replacing whatever was previously on the clipboard. With the option, your scratch work won't even be noticed by the user, and users generally appreciate that.

7.1 The Macro Editor

As you probably noticed when you were saving macros, the Bundle Editor does not allow you to edit the macros you have recorded.

Without a built-in editor, you don't want to be writing macros from scratch; however, I find that I commonly get most of the steps perfect and just need to make minor adjustments. For example, I may find an edge condition while using the macro that it could handle if I just changed a regular expression used in it. I've also run into situations where I used Filter Through Command and needed to change the shell command I passed the text through. Building a new macro just to make these changes is tedious and error-prone.

Instead, you can use TextMate as the editor. Macros are stored on your hard drive as XML documents, which is a text format you can edit. All you have to do is find the file and open it.

TextMate should keep automations you created or edited in the folder ~/Library/Application Support/TextMate/Bundles. Inside that directory there will be one or more .tmbundle folders that hold the automations for the

> ## Macro Memory
>
> Another reason you might find yourself wanting to edit a macro is to update its memory. When a macro uses a snippet, it duplicates the snippet inside the macro file. This is a defensive action taken by TextMate so it will still be able to run the macro, even if the snippet is removed. The downside is that the macro will not notice future changes you make to the snippet.
>
> If you update the snippet down the road and want the macro to evolve as well, use the macro editor technique to update the snippet copy.

named bundle.[1] Given that, you want to look inside Pragmatic Examples.tmbundle. Files will be split into folders based on the type of automation they contain. We're interested in macros for now, so you want the Macros folder.

Putting all of that together, let's edit a macro. Say you want to create a Double Number macro. The Increment Number macro you already have is close, so let's just work forward from that. Here's how to do it:

1. Open the Bundle Editor using Bundles → Bundle Editor → Show Bundle Editor (^ ⌥ ⌘ B).

2. Open the Pragmatic Examples bundle, and highlight the Increment Number macro.

3. Click the ++ button in the middle of the three action buttons in the lower-left corner of the Bundle Editor to make a copy of your macro.

4. Type Double Number to name the new macro, and switch the key equivalent to something like ^ *.

That's all you can do in the Bundle Editor, so close it. Now you need to open the macro you created so you can edit it. Choose File → Open, and navigate to ~/Library/Application Support/TextMate/Bundles/Pragmatic Examples.tmbundle/Macros/Double Number.tmMacro. Open that file.

As I said before, this is just an XML file, so you should be able to browse through it to make out the steps you executed earlier.

---

1. If you are following along in Mac OS X's Finder, they won't look like folders; however, you can ^-click a bundle and choose Show Package Contents to peek inside.

The two you are currently interested in are in this bit of the file:

`macros/double_number_before.tmMacro`

```
<dict>
        <key>argument</key>
        <string>+</string>
        <key>command</key>
        <string>insertText:</string>
</dict>
<dict>
        <key>argument</key>
        <string>1</string>
        <key>command</key>
        <string>insertText:</string>
</dict>
```

That's where I had you type + and 1 in the original macro. If you change those to * and 2, you will have made a doubler. Here's the new version of that section of the macro file:

`macros/double_number_after.tmMacro`

```
<dict>
        <key>argument</key>
        <string>*</string>
        <key>command</key>
        <string>insertText:</string>
</dict>
<dict>
        <key>argument</key>
        <string>2</string>
        <key>command</key>
        <string>insertText:</string>
</dict>
```

Close the macro file since you are done in there. Now you need to get TextMate to notice the external change to the file, so just choose Bundles → Bundle Editor → Reload Bundles. This causes TextMate to reread all the bundles as it does when it launches.

That should put you back in business with a number-doubling macro. Try it. Open a file with some numbers, click inside numbers you want to change, and trigger the macro.

The ability to record and replay your work allows you to do the tedious edits just once and leave the rest to TextMate. There's no denying how helpful that can be. However, when inserting snippets and running macros, TextMate is just copying you. Sometimes that's not quite enough and you'll find you need a little intelligence in your automated assistance. I'll tell you how to get it now.

Chapter 8

Commands

The term *command* confusingly refers to two different things in Text-Mate. First, TextMate has terrific integration with the Unix environment in Mac OS X. You can take advantage in many ways of all the Unix tools you have installed, which are generally referred to as *shell commands*.

TextMate also has a type of automation called a *command*. These often take advantage of shell commands to do their work but are really entities unto themselves. These commands are a little more capable than snippets and macros, but they require more knowledge to implement.

This chapter addresses both types of commands.

If you are not too savvy with a Unix terminal or you are not a programmer, the following is probably going to feel like wading into the deep end of the pool. You may want to skim and skip as needed in this chapter and the next. Not everyone uses these higher-level automations in TextMate.

8.1 Shell Commands

One of the key ideas that has made Unix operating systems so successful is the idea that many small pieces specializing in one little task can work together to perform powerful tasks. Mac OS X ships with all the classic Unix tools, and you can call on them when needed.

You can invoke shell commands in several ways. In Section 6.2, *Getting Snippet Data from TextMate and the Shell*, on page 86, you already examined one way to use them inside snippets. Another common usage is to fetch information from the shell while you are creating a document.

As an example, the following shell command asks ps to give you a listing of the currently active processes, which is fed to head via a Unix pipe (the | character) to trim the output to the top-ten processes:

```
ps -acux | head -n 11
```

Run that by typing the line into a TextMate editing window and clicking ⌃ R with your caret somewhere on that line. This invokes Text → Execute Line Inserting Result, and TextMate will dump the command's output right into your document.

You can even use shell commands to reach full languages, such as Perl and Python, of course. If you want to call out to Ruby, though, TextMate has a nice shortcut. Just enter some Ruby code on a line, and trigger Execute Line as Ruby from the Ruby bundle (⌃ ⇧ E). For example, the following will generate a nicely formatted random number from 1 to 100,000:

```
rand(100_000).to_s.reverse.gsub(/\d{3}/, '\0,').reverse
```

The Ruby executor is quite clever. It will inline the final results of the line executed, unless the code prints output. This allows you to use methods such as printf() to format output when needed. Also, if the result of the final line is a Ruby data structure, such as an Array or Hash, the command uses inspect() to show the Ruby code for the structure. This means you can use code to write more code.

Both of the previous commands work with a selection as well, should you need to run multiline commands.

Another way to use shell commands is to filter all or part of the current document through some commands to modify the text. For example, Mac OS X 10.4 and newer ship with a template language filter command for ERb (Embedded Ruby).

ERb allows you to mix Ruby expressions right into any document you are writing. Using ERb is simple: Any line starting with a % is treated as Ruby code and discarded from the output. You can use this to loop over output lines and set variables. You can also enter Ruby expressions between <%= %> delimiters, which will be evaluated, stringified, and inserted into the output. These two helpers make it possible to generate a lot of complex content with just a little code and template material.

Here's an example that uses ERb to generate a calendar for the current month. Enter the following code into a new TextMate document:

`commands/erb_calendar.txt`

```
% first = Date.civil(Date.today.year, Date.today.month, 1)
% last  = (first >> 1) - 1
Calendar for <%= Date::MONTHNAMES[Date.today.month] %>, <%= Date.today.year %>
+----------+----------+----------+----------+----------+----------+----------+
| Sunday   | Monday   | Tuesday  | Wednesday| Thursday | Friday   | Saturday |
% (([nil] * first.wday) + (first..last).to_a).each_slice(7) do |week|
%   week << nil while week.size < 7
+----------+----------+----------+----------+----------+----------+----------+
<%= week.map { |d| d ? "| %02d      " % d.day : "|          " } %>|
|          |          |          |          |          |          |          |
|          |          |          |          |          |          |          |
|          |          |          |          |          |          |          |
% end
+----------+----------+----------+----------+----------+----------+----------+
```

That may not look like much yet, but you can easily turn it into a full calendar. Choose Text → Filter Through Command (⌥⌘R). Note that I am speaking of the top-level Text menu here, not the Text submenu of the Bundles menu. See Figure 8.1, on the following page to learn where this command lives.

Enter erb -r date -r enumerator as the command, set up the rest of the dialog box as I have in Figure 8.2, on page 101, and click Execute. I will talk more about those input and output settings shortly, but for now the important point to notice is that I am feeding the document through a shell command and using the results to generate a new document.

For a brief introduction to some popular shell commands, see Section 9.3, *Useful Shell Commands*, on page 118.

8.2 TextMate Commands

The other kind of command in TextMate is a TextMate command, which is another form of automation like the snippets and macros I have already covered. Like shell commands, TextMate commands take input, munge the data around, and spit out some output. TextMate commands generally use shell commands.

Commands allow you to introduce some logic into your TextMate automations. This opens up all manner of possibilities for semi-intelligent assistance. For example, both the HTML and Markdown bundles have

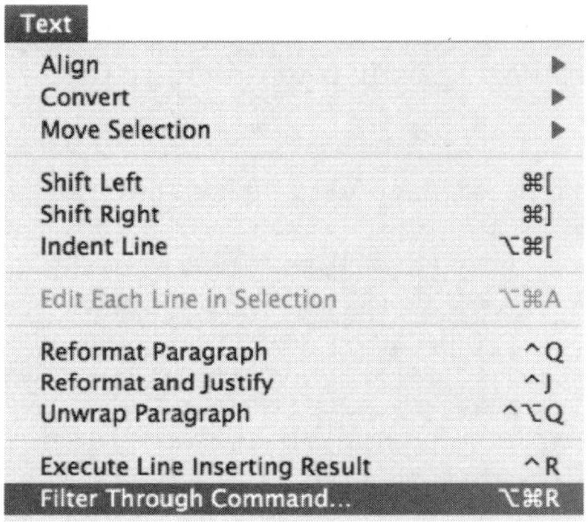

Figure 8.1: TEXT MENU

a Lookup Word on Google and Link command, which uses Google's "I'm Feeling Lucky" feature to hyperlink your text. Try it:

1. Create a new TextMate document (⌘ N).
2. Switch the document language to Markdown (press ⌃ ⌥ ⇧ M, and select Markdown).
3. Type this: TextMate.
4. Trigger the lookup command (⌃ ⇧ ⌘ L). This step requires a connection to the internet, but you can see that the insertion is a bit smarter than what you can do with a simple snippet.

To give you an idea of how to build a TextMate command, let's put one together. I work with a lot of Rails projects in my job, and I am always searching the many files of a project for some term. Most of the time I am looking for data only in Ruby source code files, but running the search in TextMate checks everything in the project, which can take a few seconds. Furthermore, I include Rails itself in the project but do not want that code to match during my searches. Let's build a tightly focused Ruby search command.

To get started, open the Bundle Editor by choosing Bundles → Bundle Editor → Show Bundle Editor (⌃ ⌥ ⌘ B), select your Pragmatic Examples bundle, and select New Command from the + menu in the lower-left corner of the window. I named the command Rails Quick Scan.

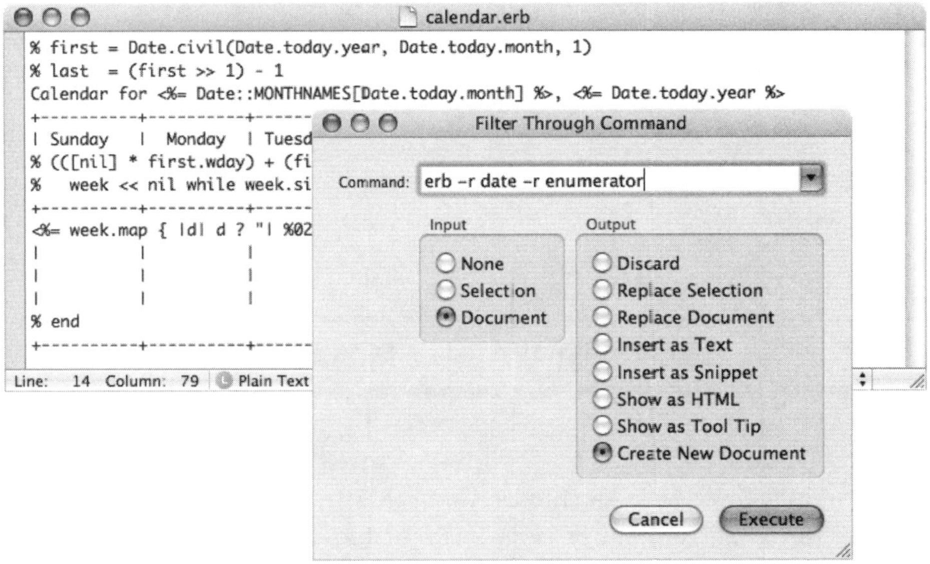

Figure 8.2: FILTER THROUGH COMMAND

Enter the following code into the Command(s) field:

`commands/quick_scan.sh`

```
echo "${TM_SELECTED_TEXT:-$TM_CURRENT_WORD}" \
| pbcopy -pboard find

cat <<END_HEAD_HTML
<html><head>
      <title>Quick Scan Results</title>
</head><body>
  <h1>Matches</h1>
  <ul>
END_HEAD_HTML

LINK='<li><a href="txmt:\/\/open?line=\4\&url=file:\/\/\1">\3<\a><\/li>'
find "${TM_PROJECT_DIRECTORY:-$TM_DIRECTORY}"   \
    \( -name "*.rb"   -or -name "*.rhtml"  -or \
       -name "*.rxml" -or -name "*.rjs" \) -or \
    \( -path './vendor' \! -prune \)           \
| xargs grep -n 'pbpaste -pboard find'         \
| sed -E 's/^(\/?([^:\/]+\/)+([^:]+)):([0-9]+):.+$/'"$LINK"'/'

cat <<END_FOOT_HTML
  </ul>
</body></html>
END_FOOT_HTML
```

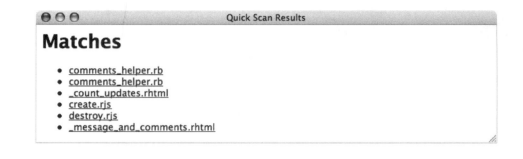

Figure 8.3: RAILS QUICK SCAN RESULTS

If you don't want to type that command without TextMate's wonderful editing tools, remember that you can use Edit in TextMate (^ ⌘ E) to open the Command(s) field in a regular TextMate editing window. This assumes you took my install advice in Section 1.4, *Installing TextMate and Tools*, on page 6.

Finish the command by setting Input to None and Output to Show as HTML. You should also specify a scope selector of source.ruby. Feel free to assign a key equivalent if you like.

If you have a Rails project around, try this command. Place your caret inside a method name or another word you would like to search for, and trigger the command by selecting it from the Pragmatic Examples submenu of the Bundles menu or by using the key equivalent you assigned. You should see the search results window shortly. If you don't have a Rails project, you will have to settle for Figure 8.3.

Now I'll cover several points about the Rails Quick Scan command. First, unless you specify otherwise, TextMate commands are assumed to be bash shell scripts. That makes it easy to string together a bunch of shell commands as I have done here: cat to write some output, pbcopy and pbpaste to place the search on the find clipboard, find to locate the Ruby files, grep to determine which files match, and sed to clean up the results.

Another point to notice here is that I have used some *TextMate environment variables* as I did in Section 6.2, *Getting Snippet Data from TextMate and the Shell*, on page 86. They work nearly the same here except that you can see I needed an extra - after the : for default values. This is just the way bash works. You also want to be sure to quote variables when working with bash scripts so their contents are not separated on whitespace like the shell is prone to do. For a list of TextMate environment variables and their uses, see Section 9.2, *TextMate's Environment Variables*, on page 113.

Finally, let's talk about a little about input and output. This command didn't need TextMate to pass it any input, because it was able to pull the needed information from the environment variables. For output, I used TextMate's powerful Show as HTML option. This has many advantages, including the ability to use hyperlinks back to TextMate as I have done here. When you click one of those links, TextMate will take you to the referenced line of the referenced file where you should see your match.

Command Input and Output

Whether you are using Filter Through Command or building a TextMate command, you need to tell TextMate what to send the command for input and what to do with the output the command generates. You have quite a few choices for both, each with unique strengths.

It's important to make sure TextMate sends you just what you need for your command. Any extra data just makes the command harder to build. Let TextMate do as much of the work getting the input as you can, before your code takes over.

With a command selected in the Bundle Editor, you can see one or two drop-down menus for setting a command's input. The left menu is always present and represents your first choice, so to speak. This menu is also the same set of input choices offered by Filter Through Command. Here are brief descriptions for the options you can select:

None
>   If you set this option, no input is sent to the command. Some commands pull the information they need from TextMate's environment variables, GUI dialog boxes presented to the user, or files on the hard disk. It's also possible that the output generated is not based on any kind of input. In these cases, you can tell TextMate that the command does not require input.

Selected Text/Selection
>   With this option, the contents of the current selection are sent to the command's standard input. Because there may not be a selection when the command is run, selecting this option exposes a fallback menu (for TextMate commands only).

Entire Document/Document

> This option sends the entire contents of the current file being edited to the command. When a command performs wholesale changes to the document contents or needs to see large portions of the document to know what needs to be done, this is how you pass the needed information.

If you are working with a TextMate command and choose Selected Text as your primary input option, you will expose the fallback menu. This menu tells TextMate what to send your command when there is no selection at the time the command is triggered. Anything sent as a backup choice counts as selected, for the purposes of output options that replace the selected text. Here are the fallback options:

Document

> The entire document is sent to the command's standard input stream.

Line

> The complete line the caret is on is sent to the command, without a terminating line-end character.

Word

> The run of word characters the caret is immediately before, immediately after, or inside of is sent to the command.

Character

> The character to the right of the caret is sent to the command.

Scope

> This option can be a powerful means to work with TextMate content. When triggered, TextMate will search forward and backward from the caret for the first point where the scope of the document would change. Everything inside those boundaries is sent to the command. This makes it possible to write commands that deal with things such as XML tag content or literal string declarations in source code files, because their delimiters will introduce a new scope.
>
> For another way to access document content with TextMate scoping information, see Section 9.4, *Using TextMate's Document Parsing*, on page 123.

Nothing

> The command does not receive any input from TextMate.

It's important to remember that even with a fallback specified, it's possible for your command to receive no input. A document or line can be empty, the caret may not be touching a word, and so on.

If you set a fallback selection, you can take advantage of another TextMate nicety. If your command name includes text such as "Fallback/Selection," TextMate will adjust the command name when it is used in menus. When no text is selected in the editing window, the word before the slash appears. If there is a selection, TextMate will use the word *Selection*. For example, the Text bundle includes a command called Duplicate Line/Selection, but if you go into the menu to find it, you will see either Duplicate Line or Duplicate Selection depending on whether a selection appears in the editing window.

TextMate commands also have an input-related feature at the top of the Bundle Editor. Using the Save drop-down menu, you can specify that the current file, or even all files in the project, are saved to the hard disk before the command is run. This is important for commands such as Show TODO List that need to scan the files to do their work. Turning this option on can make sure the files you scan are up-to-date. Users prefer to have control over when they save files, though, so I recommend using this option sparingly and only when you truly need it.

The other half of the equation is getting data back from a command and specifying what exactly you want TextMate to do with it. You can define this for TextMate commands in the Bundle Editor with the Output drop-down menu. When you are working with Filter Through Command, you can find these settings on the right half dialog box.

Take some time to consider your output options when building a command because it can dramatically affect how useful the command is to you in the long run. Are you filtering content and wanting to replace the old with the new, are you generating new content altogether, or do you just need to see some information before you continue editing? Each of these scenarios has multiple options. Here's a breakdown of the different options:

Discard

Selecting this causes TextMate to ignore any output generated by the command. This isn't a common choice but might be useful for commands that have side effects such as creating files on the hard disk to be edited.

Replace Selected Text/Replace Selection

> The user's current selection is replaced by the generated output. Remember that fallback selections will be replaced when using this option.

Replace Document

> For commands that rewrite the entire document, this option allows a command to replace the contents of the editing window.

Insert as Text

> Instead of replacing some part of the document, command output is simply inserted at the caret location using this option.

Insert as Snippet

> This is a powerful choice that makes all the snippet tools available to the output a command inserts. This allows commands to programmatically introduce tab triggers where they are needed.
>
> Commands often use this option merely to set where the caret appears in the output by adding a $0 (or ${0} to be safe when you are unsure whether it will appear with other digits) at the desired location. Commands that generate snippet output need to remember to escape special snippet characters such as $ and ` in their output.
>
> Insert as Snippet has other advantages as well. First, it will replace a selection if there is one, just as Replace Selected Text does. Furthermore, TextMate will reindent inserted snippet content to match the current indent level of the document in which it is placed.

Show as HTML

> TextMate's HTML output window is a high-powered display tool. Output can use any combination of HTML and CSS to present the user with pleasantly formatted results. Commands using this option should just print a complete web page to their standard output stream.
>
> One advantage of this output format is the ability to hyperlink to files. With a properly composed link, you can ask TextMate to open the named file in an editor window or just bring the file to the front if it was already open. You can even take the user right to a line in the file if desired. TextMate links are easy enough to build; just create a typical HTML link with a URL of the form

txmt://open?url=file:// followed by the complete path to the file (URL escaped). If you would like to target a line in the file, add &line= followed by a line number after the file path.

When building HTML commands for TextMate, it is sometimes helpful to see the source markup that was rendered. TextMate has a View Source command in the View menu to help developers with this, and it has the same keyboard shortcut Safari uses for the same feature: ⌥⌘U.

For more advantages of the HTML output window, see Section 9.8, *Streaming Command Output*, on page 130 and Section 9.9, *Building Interactive Commands*, on page 133.

Show as Tool Tip

This is an unobtrusive option for commands that just need to briefly flash a little feedback in front of the user. All generated output will appear in a tooltip near the current caret location. The tooltip fades as soon as the user returns to editing.

Create New Document

With this option selected, a new editing window is created, and all output from the command is used as the initial content for this window. This is generally used by commands that convert from one document format to another, allowing the user to do whatever is needed with the converted content while holding on to the original material.

Using Ruby or Another Scripting Language

bash is nice when you just need to pipe some data through commands. It also elegantly handles stream redirection. Whenever I start needing moderately complex logic for a command, though, I would rather use a scripting language. Luckily, you can do just that.

If the first line of a TextMate command is a shebang line, the following code can be in the language understood by the indicated interpreter. In other words, you can write a TextMate command in Perl if the first line is as follows:

```
#!/usr/bin/env perl
```

I generally use the following to ask for Ruby and turn on warnings:

```
#!/usr/bin/env ruby -w
```

As an example, let's look at a full TextMate command written in Ruby. This example comes again from my Rails work, but it's liable to be helpful to anyone who works with YAML files. In Rails it's common to write test fixtures, which are really just arrays of hashes in a YAML file format. I got tired of repeating all the keys and having to generate the Rails ID fields, so I asked TextMate to do it for me:

```ruby
commands/build_fixtures.rb
#!/usr/bin/env ruby -w

require "#{ENV["TM_SUPPORT_PATH"]}/lib/dialog"

count  = Dialog.request_string( :prompt  => "How many fixtures do you need?",
                                :button1 => "OK" ).to_i
fields = Dialog.request_string( :prompt  => "Please enter non-id fields " +
                                            "separated by commas:",
                                :button1 => "OK" ).split(/,\s*/)

puts "---"
count.times do |i|
  puts "name_me:"
  puts "  id: #{i + 1}"
  puts fields.map { |f| "  #{f.strip}:" }
end
```

Dump that code into the body of a new command. I called my version Build YAML Fixtures. Set Input to Selected Text or Entire Document, and set Output to Replace Selected Text. You should also give the command a scope selector of source.yaml. As always, feel free to assign a key equivalent.

To test-drive this command, create an empty YAML document, and trigger the command. Feed the first dialog box that shows up a positive integer and the second one some field names such as login, password, email. At that point the command should spit out a skeleton YAML structure you could fill in as needed.

Aside from the language change, this example has another interesting aspect. It loads one of the TextMate support libraries and uses that to fetch information from the user via GUI dialog boxes. TextMate has several of these support libraries you are free to use, and you can read more about them in Section 9.5, *bash Support Functions*, on page 125 and Section 9.6, *Ruby Support Libraries*, on page 127.

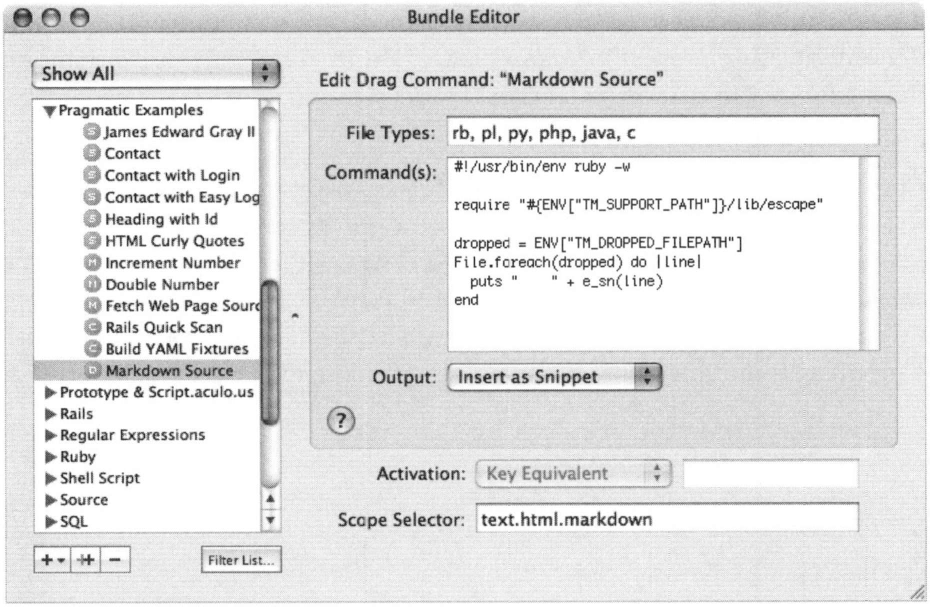

Figure 8.4: MARKDOWN SOURCE DRAG COMMAND

8.3 Drag Commands

TextMate has another kind of command you can create in the Bundle Editor called a *drag command*. You activate a drag command when you drag and drop a file onto a TextMate document and the file matches one of the types handled by the drag command.

Drag commands work like regular commands, save that they do not receive input. They can access the dropped file using environment variables. Drag commands are also limited to one kind of output: Insert as Snippet.

To give an example of where they can be useful, I'll tell you about my Markdown Source drag command. I frequently write about source code, so it's common for me to drag code files into documents I'm editing. TextMate will insert the contents at the drop point normally, but with Markdown source needs to be indented so it will format correctly. To handle that, I built a drag command that indents the source for me. You can see the entire command in Figure 8.4.

This command just inserts each line of the dropped file into the current document after prepending four spaces to it. Note that the command does escape the document content, since you must insert it as a snippet. The escaping is handled with another TextMate support library.

Commands are powerful tools for those who want to go all the way down the rabbit hole of automation. You may not need to go this far, or at least not too often, but a well-designed command can certainly help the workflow move forward. This is the final form of TextMate automation. I've covered a lot of ground with them, so I'll next give you a few more general automation tips before you should consider the subject closed.

Chapter 9

Automation Tips and Tricks

You now know how to build three kinds of automations for TextMate, but you can still learn a lot of tricks for using them effectively. You will pick these up over time as you create automations, but I'll jump-start your learning process by showing you some favorite techniques used by the TextMate gurus. This material can take you above the novice automator ranks and give you the ability to build powerful custom tools to handle your unique workflow.

You may not ever need some of these tips, and you certainly won't need them all at once. I recommend skimming this chapter to get an idea of what's covered and then referencing the material later when you are trying to accomplish a related task. I've tried to lay out the information to support this pattern of usage.

9.1 Building Bundle Menus

No one wants to scan through a menu hunting for the automation that does what they need. As a bundle grows, selecting automations from one long list becomes tedious. For that reason, TextMate gives you the ability to organize a bundle's menu with submenus and dividers.

You access the menu-building interface by choosing Bundles → Bundle Editor → Show Bundle Editor (^ ⌥ ⌘ B) and clicking the name of the bundle you want to organize. The Menu Structure box contains all the items in the bundle in their menu order and layout. Excluded Items serves two purposes, which will become clear as you move forward through this chapter.

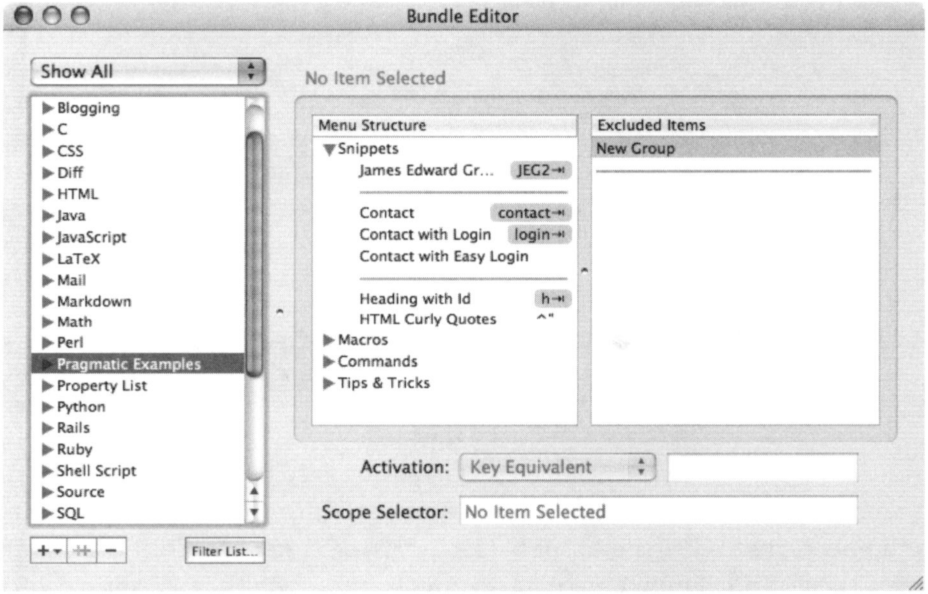

Figure 9.1: BUNDLE MENU STRUCTURE

Here are the changes you can make to the menu structure:

- Reorder automations as they will appear in the Bundles menu by dragging the automation name and dropping it where you want it to be listed.
- Add dividers to a menu by dragging the divider line from Excluded Items and dropping it into position.
- Create a new submenu by dragging the New Group label out of Excluded Items and dropping it in the menu for which you want to create a submenu.
- Rename a menu item, including newly created submenus, by double-clicking the item name to expose the editor and typing a new name.
- Unfold a submenu so you can arrange its contents by clicking the triangle just to the left of the submenu's name until it points straight down.

Try organizing your Pragmatic Examples bundle to get the hang of these features. You should pick it up in no time. You can see an example of my menu structure in Figure 9.1.

You can also drag automations from Menu Structure into Excluded Items. This will hide them so they do not appear in the Bundles menu. You can still activate automations in Excluded Items using the item's key equivalent or tab trigger. You may want to stick items in here that make sense to activate only via the keyboard (as opposed to using the Bundles menu). Just make sure the user has some way of knowing that the item is there at all. You can also use Excluded Items to depreciate automations you plan to remove from the bundle down the line.

Remember that the point of a good menu structure is to guide the user right to what they want to find. Users are lazy and impatient, so make sure the menus divide the available automations into a logical grouping of an easily digested size.

9.2 TextMate's Environment Variables

Both snippets and commands have access to a collection of environment variables when they run. TextMate sets up most of these variables for you, but you are free to set your own variables and use them in your automations.

To set a variable that will be used in all automations, add the variable's name and value to the Shell Variables list under TextMate → Preferences (⌘ ,). You can reach the list by clicking the Advanced icon at the top of the preferences window and then selecting the Shell Variables tab, as shown in Figure 9.2, on the following page.

You can also set project-level variables used only for automations run on the files of that project. To reach the semi-hidden interface for this, select View → Show Project Drawer (^ ⌥ ⌘ D) unless it is already visible, make sure nothing is selected in the drawer (click the whitespace if you need to deselect items), and click the i button in the lower-right corner of the project drawer.

The SQL bundle is a great example of how these variables might be useful to you. I have TM_DB_SERVER set to mysql in my TextMate preferences, so the bundle knows which database I favor. Then, inside each database-oriented project I work with, I set MYSQL_USER to my login name for MySQL (defaults to your Mac OS X login name), MYSQL_PWD to my password, and MYSQL_DB to the database I am working with.[1]

---

1. If you are a Postgres fan, consult Bundles → SQL → Help for details on how to set up that database server.

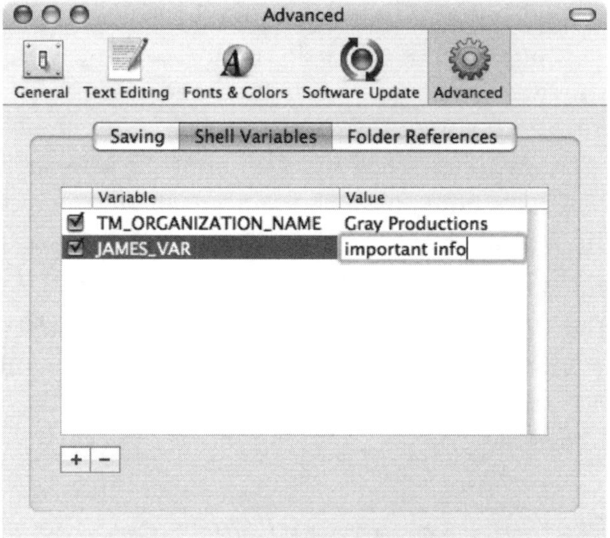

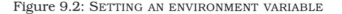

Figure 9.2: SETTING AN ENVIRONMENT VARIABLE

With that set up, I can select any SQL query in my project and choose Bundles → SQL → Execute Selection as Query (^ ⇧ Q) to have TextMate display the results. That's a convenient way to reality check database contents while you work without needing to leave TextMate.

Here's a list of the variables TextMate maintains for you and suggestions about how you might use them:

TM_BUNDLE_SUPPORT

When you write a small command, it's fine to crack open the Bundle Editor, jot down some code, and try it. More complicated commands require better organization, though, and you might want to share some code or other resources among a group of related commands. TextMate supports this through this variable.

If the bundle a command is called from contains a top-level Support folder, this variable will point to that folder. You can use this to locate the needed external resources.

For example, to use an external library in a bundle you are building, create a Support/lib directory in the bundle, add the library you need to this directory, and require the library in your command with code similar to this Ruby example:

```
require "#{ENV['TM_BUNDLE_SUPPORT']}/lib/external_library"
```

Another perk of the Support folder is that Support/bin is added to the path while a command executes. This ensures that you don't even need this variable to reach external programs, as long as you place them in this folder.

TM_SUPPORT_PATH

The TextMate application also contains a Support folder including several programs, code libraries, and other resources useful in developing automations. This variable always points to the root of that directory, so you can load TextMate's GUI dialog box support library with the following line of Ruby:

```
require "#{ENV["TM_SUPPORT_PATH"]}/lib/dialog"
```

Again, the bin directory of this folder is added to the path while a command executes. This allows you to shell out to bundled commands, including CocoaDialog, Markdown.pl, Textile.rb, and more, from any automation.

TM_CURRENT_LINE
TM_CURRENT_WORD
TM_SELECTED_TEXT

These variables function just like the fallback menu equivalents for command input described in Section 8.2, *Command Input and Output*, on page 103. Environment variables do have a size limit, which can cause the data in these variables to be truncated in extreme cases. Therefore, it's better to have these sent to your command as input.

TM_SCOPE

This is the scope the caret is currently inside. The Show Scope command of the TextMate bundle prints the contents of this variable as a tooltip.

TM_LINE_INDEX
TM_LINE_NUMBER

These variables are indices into the document being edited. TM_LINE_INDEX is a zero-based count to the current caret location in the line. This variable is aware of the line encoding and thus will count multibyte characters correctly. TM_LINE_NUMBER is the line of the document the caret is currently on, counting from one. In a Ruby command that is sent the document as input, you could use code like the following to examine the text around the caret:

```
doc     = ARGF.readlines
line_no = ENV['TM_LINE_NUMBER'].to_i
line    = doc[line_no - 1]
line_i  = ENV['TM_LINE_INDEX'].to_i

puts "Line before caret:  #{line[0...line_i]}"
puts "Line after caret:  #{line[line_i..-1]}"
```

TM_INPUT_START_LINE
TM_INPUT_START_LINE_INDEX

These variables provide offsets describing where the input sent to your command began in the document. Among other uses, you can use them to locate the caret's position inside the input you received using code like the following:

```
# set line and col with the indices for the caret in the input
line = ENV['TM_LINE_NUMBER'].to_i - ENV['TM_INPUT_START_LINE'].to_i
col  = ENV['TM_LINE_INDEX'].to_i
if ENV['TM_LINE_NUMBER'].to_i == ENV['TM_INPUT_START_LINE'].to_i
  col -= ENV['TM_INPUT_START_LINE_INDEX'].to_i
end
```

TM_COLUMN_NUMBER
TM_COLUMNS

You can use these variables to find the current column location of the caret (counting from one) and the number of columns available in the editing window, assuming Soft Wrap is active. You might prefer TM_COLUMN_NUMBER to the previously mentioned TM_LINE_INDEX in places where you want to know exactly where the caret is. For example, if you are trying to find the indent level where the command is triggered, TM_LINE_INDEX may tell you that you are two characters in, but if those characters happen to be tabs, TM_COLUMN_NUMBER holds exactly how far into the line you are, accounting for the current tab size.

TM_TAB_SIZE
TM_SOFT_TABS

If you need to mimic user settings for indention in some command output, these two variables are helpful. TM_TAB_SIZE will tell you the current size of a tab in the editing window, and TM_SOFT_TABS will tell you whether those tabs are being represented as actual tab characters (variable set to NO or unset) or as the equivalent number of spaces (a YES setting). Since you can't count on what TM_SOFT_TABS will be when tabs are used, always test for the YES value.

TM_DIRECTORY
TM_PROJECT_DIRECTORY
TM_FILEPATH

You can use these variables to locate the directory containing the currently active file, the top-level project directory for the project containing the file, and the current file itself. It's important to note that these variables may not be set. The user may not have a project open, and the current document may not yet be saved to the disk.

If you need document content, it's better to set up the command input to send you what you need than to try to read it using these variables. The user may have unsaved changes that wouldn't be reflected in the disk file. Still, these variables can be useful for fetching information from the file system or manipulating files based on their location. See Section 9.7, *Hooking Into Save Operations*, on page 128 for details about a kind of command that might need these variables.

TM_SELECTED_FILE
TM_SELECTED_FILES

You can use these variables to find out what is currently selected in the project drawer, assuming the user is working with a project and there is currently a selection of files and folders in the drawer. The singular variable gives only the path to the first selected item, and the second gives a shell-escaped listing of all currently selected files. If you would like to get these files into an Array inside a Ruby command, use the following code:

```
require "shellwords"
```

```
selected = Shellwords.shellwords(ENV["TM_SELECTED_FILES"])
```

TM_DROPPED_FILE
TM_DROPPED_FILEPATH
TM_MODIFIER_FLAGS

This family of variables is populated only during the execution of a drag command. You use these variables as your primary means of interacting with the dropped file.

TM_DROPPED_FILE holds a relative path to the file from TM_DIRECTORY. I find it easier to work with an absolute path most of the time, and you can find that in TM_DROPPED_FILEPATH.

When a file is dragged onto a TextMate document, the user may choose to hold down one or more modifier keys on the keyboard. If your command needs to react to these keys, you can find out what was held with the variable TM_MODIFIER_FLAGS. The variable holds a string like "SHIFT|CONTROL|OPTION|COMMAND", assuming all options are pressed. To check for an option using Ruby, you can write this:

```
if ENV["TM_MODIFIER_FLAGS"].include? "OPTION"
  # handle option key pressed here
else
  # handle option key not pressed here
end
```

If you would like to spot-check the variables your command will be passed when invoked, run the Show TM_* Variables command in the TextMate submenu of the Bundles menu in place of the command you would have run. A tooltip will appear with the name and contents of the variables that would have been passed to your command.

9.3 Useful Shell Commands

Between the files stored on the hard drive and what the operating system itself knows, a lot of data is available to snippets and commands. Shell commands are the gateway to that data, and learning how to use them can really give a boost to your text-editing abilities.

For example, signing any generated content with the name of the current user is as easy as shelling out to the Directory Service utility to get the name, and you can throw in a call to sed to clean it up:

```
dscl . read /Users/$USER realname | sed -E 's/^realname: +//'
```

Mac OS X ships with hundreds of applications accessible from the shell. I couldn't begin to tell you what they all do, but here are a handful of commands that are handy to know when editing text, manipulating files, working with the operating system, or even just for learning about other commands:

cat

> This utility outputs files given as arguments or the data it receives on STDIN. You could use this to insert content directly into Text-Mate documents with commands such as cat /usr/share/dict/words.

curl

> If you want to manage some network communication from the command line, curl is your best friend. It knows most popular protocols including HTTP and FTP. You can use this to check the availability of a network resource (curl -I http://rubyquiz.com), fetch the entire resource (curl http://rubyquiz.com), download files (curl -O http://media.pragprog.com/titles/textmate/code/textmate-code.tgz), or fill out web forms:

```
curl -d 'command=sum+1+2+3+4+5' -g -L http://yubnub.org/parser/parse
```

echo

> Use this to generate a line of content just by passing the line as a command-line argument. For example, use echo 'A line to output'. This command is also a handy way to find the current value of a TextMate environment variable: echo $TM_FILEPATH.

find

> This shell command will walk a file hierarchy and return the path to all files matching certain criteria. You could use this to get a list of all Ruby files below the current directory, for example, with a call such as find . -name *.rb.

fmt

> You can use this formatter to wrap lines at a specified length. This can be helpful in TextMate to restrict command output to a given width: cat unwraped_document.txt | fmt -w 80.

grep

> By feeding grep a regular expression, you can restrict output to only the lines of a file or STDIN that match the provided expression. For example, use cat todo_list.txt | grep -E '^ *TODO'.
>
> Use the -v switch to invert the results to show the unmatched lines. This can be a slick way to prune document content with Filter Through Command (⌥ ⌘ R).

> ### Unix Regular Expressions
>
> Many shell commands can use regular expressions. I often use them with find, grep, and sed.
>
> Be warned, though—the regular expressions these commands accept are not as powerful as TextMate's regular expression engine. Passing an -E flag to these commands will activate their "extended" syntax, which is pretty close to what I covered for TextMate.
>
> Avoid using shortcut character classes such as \d and advanced features such as look-arounds and conditional replacements. The basic elements are the same, though.
>
> You can learn more by feeding Terminal the command man re_format.

head
tail

> These tools are for looking at the first n lines of a file or STDIN (cat email.txt | head -n 4) or the last n lines (cat error.log | tail -n 10). Just pass the number of lines needed after the -n switch. These commands are often used to examine document headers or the latest entries of log files.
>
> When you are working with something like a log, you may be more interested in the newest lines, which are generally at the end of the stream. In this case, the -r switch supported by tail to reverse the lines is helpful to know.

iconv

> Use this tool to convert files of one encoding to another. You pass iconv from and to encoding names with command-line switches: iconv -f ISO_8859-1 -t UTF-8 old_file.txt.

man

> This command will open the manual pages for other shell commands. You probably won't use this in TextMate too much, but you can use it to look up documentation for all the commands covered here and more. Just name the command you would like to read the documentation for in the call: man curl.

mdfind

mdls

> You can use this pair of commands to perform Spotlight searches from the command line. To see all the metadata associated with a given file, just hand the filename to mdls with a call like mdls stock_report.doc.
>
> To perform full Spotlight searches, you need mdfind. You can use that tool to perform simple searches among all metadata fields, as the Spotlight tool in the menu bar does, with calls such as mdfind Rails. You can also perform searches targeting specific fields of metadata with calls such as mdfind "kMDItemFSName == 'test.rb'".

osascript

> This tool will allow you to communicate with Apple's AppleScript environment and through that give instructions to many Mac applications. For example, you could play the current system sound with osascript -e beep.

pbcopy

pbpaste

> You can use these commands to place data on and retrieve data from Mac OS X's paste board, known to most users as the *clipboard*. You could add a line to the clipboard with this:

```
echo 'http://www.pragmaticprogrammer.com/' | pbcopy
```

> and later fetch it back with pbpaste.
>
> Mac OS X has a separate clipboard for search patterns used in Find dialog boxes. These commands can affect that clipboard with the -pboard find option. You may want to use this to generate search patterns for the TextMate Find dialog box.
>
> These commands default to the default encoding of the system (MacRoman for Western users), so you should switch to UTF-8 before using these commands for any non-ASCII content. You can make the change by having your command execute the following before you call pbcopy or pbpaste:

```
export __CF_USER_TEXT_ENCODING=$UID:0x8000100:0x8000100
```

> Tempting though it may be, do not stick that line in your shell start-up scripts. It can cause some programs to misbehave.

perl
php
python

> You've seen me using Ruby just about everywhere in this book because that's my scripting weapon of choice. I use it often when shelling out to introduce moderately complex logic. Of course, if you're a fan of another scripting language, such as those listed previously, you can use it to do the same.

sed

> This is a terrific tool for quick data transformations. sed supports many options for changing the input passed through it including regular expression search and replace: echo "I have three dogs and two cats." | sed -E 's/[AEIOUaeiou]/X/g'.

sort

> You can use this command to order a collection of lines from a file or STDIN. Commands may need this to provide a human with friendly ordering of command output. For example, use sort names.txt.

tee

> A poor man's backup, this command can duplicate a Unix stream. It is usually used to dump some data to a file and continue processing: echo '^config=.+' | tee find_pattern.txt | pbcopy -pboard find.

touch

> This tool is actually intended to update a file's modification time so tools such as compilers will examine the file again. It sees at least as much use, though, in creating blank files. This might be helpful to TextMate commands wanting to initialize some directory structure with files to be edited: touch plugin.rb test.rb.

uniq

> This command will remove duplicate adjacent lines from a file or STDIN. This is helpful when you generate a lot of data but need only a single entry for each line. Since it catches only adjacent lines, you generally want to sort the data first to bring like lines together: cat event_days.txt | sort | uniq.

uuidgen

> This command is helpful anytime you need to generate a unique ID. Different computers and different times of execution will affect the ID generated, so it's safe to count on them being unique.

xargs

> It's common to programmatically build up arguments to a shell command and have xargs pass them on to the command in question. xargs will separate STDIN on whitespace and forward each chunk of data it finds as an argument to the named utility. For example, you could use this to build a find command that will match a name pattern currently on the clipboard with pbpaste -pboard find | xargs find . -name.

xxd

> If you want to make sense of a binary data file, this tool is often invaluable. xxd will create a hex dump for the passed file, which you can then examine in an editor such as TextMate: xxd codex.umz | mate.

9.4 Using TextMate's Document Parsing

You've already seen how TextMate can send all manner of input to the commands you write; but instead of getting raw text, you can also ask TextMate to tell you how it parses the text. This can make it easier to find the pieces of a document you need to see, since TextMate breaks them down for you. I'll now show you how this works.

First, let's create a command that just returns the input it receives and set that input to be the entire document. You can place the output in a new window. The body of the command is one word: cat. Open any document, run your new creation, and verify that TextMate makes a duplicate of the document in a new window.

Not impressed yet? Just wait until you see my next trick....

To activate parsed input, you must make a change to the actual command file on your hard disk. You'll use the same technique as in Section 7.1, *The Macro Editor*, on page 94.

I named my command Show Parsed Input, so I have to edit the file ~/Library/Application Support/TextMate/Bundles/Pragmatic Examples.tmbundle /Commands/Show Parsed Input.tmCommand. Just choose File → Open and navigate to the document.

To change the behavior of the command, add these two magic lines just before the closing </dict> tag:

```
<key>inputFormat</key>
<string>xml</string>
```

These lines adjust a hidden setting for the command. By setting it to xml, you tell TextMate that you are prepared to receive extra information with the passed text, in the form of XML markup.

Save the file, close it, and ask TextMate to reread it by choosing Bundles → Bundle Editor → Reload Bundles.

Open any document that TextMate will syntax highlight, and run your command one more time. This time you should receive your document content decorated in XMLish markup showing the scopes into which TextMate has divided the document. I say "XMLish" because the scope names don't make good XML tag names. However, the document content is properly escaped, and you can easily turn it into something you can work with using this Ruby code:

```ruby
xml = ARGF.read.gsub(/<(.*?)>/) do |tag|
  if    tag.size == 2 then ""
  elsif tag[1]   == ?/ then "</scope>"
  else                     "<scope name='#{$1}'>"
  end
end
```

Once you have a structure like that, you can load an XML library and hunt down what you want with XPath searches. Here's a sample command that uses TextMate's ability to parse Ruby source code to present the user with an outline of classes and the methods they contain:

`automation_tips_and_tricks/show_class_structure.rb`

```ruby
#!/usr/bin/env ruby -w

require "rexml/document"

xml = ARGF.read.gsub(/<(.*?)>/) do |tag|
  if    tag.size == 2 then ""
  elsif tag[1]   == ?/ then "</scope>"
  else                     "<scope name='#{$1}'>"
  end
end
doc = REXML::Document.new(xml)

met, cla = "entity.name.function.ruby", "entity.name.type.class.ruby"
doc.elements.each("//scope[@name='#{met}' or @name='#{cla}']") do |tag|
  if tag.attributes["name"] == cla
    puts tag.text
  else
    puts "  " + tag.text
  end
end
```

Open the Bundle Editor (^ ⌥ ⌘ B), create a new command with that code in the Command(s) field, set Input to Entire Document, and set Output to Create New Document. It needs to be scoped to source.ruby, and you will need to open the command file TextMate saves to the hard disk to add the XML input lines.

Once you have it set up, try running it on some Ruby libraries. Mac OS X ships with standard Ruby libraries you can use. For example, try running it on /usr/lib/ruby/1.8/set.rb.

9.5 bash Support Functions

Before TextMate runs a bash command, it triggers an internal script to set up the environment for you. This does some nice things, such as setting up the path as I described in Section 9.2, *TextMate's Environment Variables*, on page 113. It also defines a handful of functions you can use in your command.

First, require_cmd will allow you to check whether a shell command is in the path and thus available for use. If the shell command is not found, an error is reported to the user, and your command aborts. It's a good idea to call this before using a shell command that does not ship with Mac OS X so you can make sure the user has installed it. You may even want to check for commands that don't ship with all versions of the operating system, just in case the user has a different version. If you wanted to check for mysqldump, for example, before using it to dump a database table into an SQL file, you would enter this:

```
require_cmd mysqldump
```

Another family of useful functions are those that allow you to change the output type of your command. It's common for commands to check the conditions they were run under and then bail out with an error message if a requirement is missing. You don't need to create a new document just to show a small error message, even if that is the command's regular output. In such a case, you can change the output format with something like this:

```
exit_show_tool_tip "Sorry, this command only works between 8 AM and 5 PM."
```

The user will see your message, as a tooltip in this case, and the command will exit. This works for all commands except those set to HTML output, so remember to switch to HTML instead of away from it.

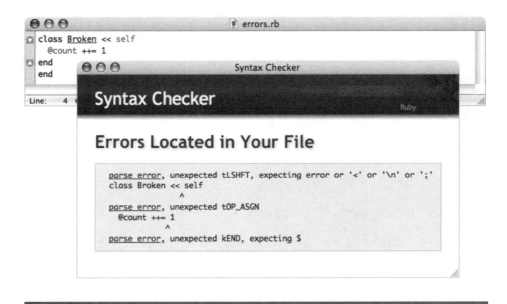

Figure 9.3: SYNTAX CHECKER

Here's the complete list of exit functions corresponding to the available command outputs:

- exit_discard
- exit_replace_text
- exit_replace_document
- exit_insert_text
- exit_insert_snippet
- exit_show_html
- exit_show_tool_tip
- exit_create_new_document

TextMate doesn't usually reflect changes to files and directories in the project drawer after a command runs, but you can use another function to get around that. If your command creates, moves, or deletes files and directories, end it with a call to rescan_project so TextMate will pick up the changes.

Finally, if you want to output the themed HTML pages used by so many of TextMate's commands (see Figure 9.3, for a peek at such styling), you can load another file to gain access to the support functions.

Here's a skeleton command to get you started with styled HTML output:

automation_tips_and_tricks/styled_html.sh

```
source "$TM_SUPPORT_PATH/lib/webpreview.sh"
html_header "Header Goes Here" "Subheader Here"

echo "<p>Your content goes here...</p>"
cat <<END_PRE | pre
you can
  even include
    <escaped> content
      using the
        pre helper
END_PRE

html_footer
```

9.6 Ruby Support Libraries

TextMate also includes several Ruby support libraries. You will find some of the same functions, and more, offered in bash within these libraries. To load any of the Ruby helpers, you need to make sure the directory they are located in is in the path. To do that, add the following line to the top of your script (before require statements):

```
$LOAD_PATH << "#{ENV["TM_SUPPORT_PATH"]}/lib"
```

The Ruby equivalents to the bash functions for changing command output modes are in the exit_codes.rb library. You can require it normally after modifying the path as I described previously and then call any of the exit methods listed in Section 9.5, *bash Support Functions*, on page 125, on the TextMate module loaded by the code.

You will also find Ruby equivalents to the styled HTML helpers in web_preview.rb. The methods have the same names as their bash counterparts. See Section 9.7, *Hooking Into Save Operations*, on the next page for an example using both of these libraries.

Another helpful Ruby library is escape.rb. It loads a handful of methods that you can filter Strings through to escape them for various uses. The provided methods are as follows:

e_sh()

> Returns an escaped version of the passed argument that can be safely used in the shell (as a single term).

e_sn()

> Returns an escaped version of the passed argument that has all special characters for TextMate snippets escaped.

e_as()

> Returns an escaped version of the passed argument that can be safely used in an AppleScript string.

e_url()

> Returns a URL-escaped version of the passed argument.

htmlize()

> Escapes the HTML entities in the passed argument and switches line endings to <br> tags, as described in Section 9.8, *Streaming Command Output*, on page 130. This method also adds some special whitespace handling to ensure that the document formatting is preserved when you place the content inside <pre style="white-space: normal;">...</pre> tags.

Another good Ruby add-on is textmate.rb. It loads several methods, but probably the most helpful are TextMate.each_text_file() and TextMate.selected_files(). The former will **yield** each text file of the current project to a block you provide, similar to the each() iterator that Rubyists are so used to using. The latter returns an Array of the files and directories selected in the project drawer.

Additionally, TextMate ships with bundled copies of some favorite Ruby libraries including bluecloth.rb, Builder.rb, redcloth.rb, and rubypants.rb.

9.7 Hooking Into Save Operations

Some applications give you hooks for running code on certain built-in operations. Save is a common target for extra functionality, because people always want to perform clever tasks such as copying a file to a server when it changes. Officially, TextMate doesn't provide any tools for this, but all the pieces are there if you just adjust your thinking enough to see how they fit together—well, for the Save command when triggered by the keyboard at least.

The trick is simple enough once someone explains it. You can hook into Save with the following formula:

1. Create a new command that will hold your post-Save code.
2. Set the command's Save field to Current File.
3. Scope the command as tightly as possible so it will affect only the saves you really want it to affect.
4. Give the command a key equivalent of ⌘ S.

TextMate will honor your key equivalents over its own predefined keyboard shortcuts, so the previous actually overrides the regular Save functionality. However, we told the command to save before it does anything else, which restores the overridden functionality with the added bonus that the code in the command runs just after the save.

Here's an example to show what you might do with something like this. The following command will syntax check a Ruby file whenever you save it. When found, you will be shown the errors Ruby reported in your syntax. This won't catch all the problems, of course, but it does make a nice early-warning system. See Figure 9.3, on page 126, for an example error listing. Follow the previous steps to set up a command called Check Ruby Syntax and scope it to source.ruby. Finally, dump this code in as the body of the command:

`automation_tips_and_tricks/save_hook.rb`

```ruby
#!/usr/bin/env ruby -w

$LOAD_PATH << "#{ENV["TM_SUPPORT_PATH"]}/lib"
require "exit_codes"
require "web_preview"
require "escape"

check = `ruby -c 2>&1`

if check.include? "Syntax OK"
  puts check
else
  file = ENV["TM_FILEPATH"]
  check = htmlize(check)
  check.gsub!( /(^|<br>)-:(\d+):\s+([\w\s]+)/,
               "\\1<a href='txmt://open?url=file://#{file}&line=\\2'>\\3</a>" )
  html_header("Syntax Checker", "Ruby")
  puts <<END_HTML
<h1>Errors Located in Your File</h1>
<pre style="white-space: normal;">#{check}</pre>
END_HTML
  html_footer
  TextMate.exit_show_html
end
```

That command needs the document as input, and it should have its output set to a tooltip. In truth, it uses the tooltip only when the code is OK. If there are errors, it will ask TextMate to switch to the HTML display so it can present a hyperlinked error list. You always want to switch to HTML like this when you need it, because you can't switch away from HTML output. Once TextMate displays the HTML window, you're committed.

This command is also a pretty good example of just how much work you can get done with TextMate's support libraries, described in Section 9.6, *Ruby Support Libraries*, on page 127. Automation is all about getting TextMate to do as much as possible for you, even when writing the automations yourself. Remember to use the tools available to you.

9.8 Streaming Command Output

Some commands take a little time to run, and you don't want the user to be left waiting until everything is finished to see what happened. You deal with this by streaming output to users as it is available so they can follow the progress of the command. TextMate commands can do this using the Show as HTML output option, but you can use a couple of tricks when streaming output.

The good news is that streaming is pretty automatic when using Show as HTML. The output will usually just appear in the window as it becomes available. To see how this works, create a new command with Input set to None and Output set to Show as HTML, and then enter the following code as the body of the command:

`automation_tips_and_tricks/streaming.rb`

```
#!/usr/bin/env ruby -w

STDOUT.sync = true  # flush output as we write it

puts <<END_HTML_START
<html><head>
  <title>A Streaming Command</title>
</head><body>
  <p>This should appear as soon as the command starts...</p>
END_HTML_START

sleep 1  # pause for one second

puts "  <p>This should appear one second later...</p>"
```

```
sleep 2  # pause for two seconds

puts <<END_HTML_END
  <p>Finally, this should appear about three second into execution.</p>
</body><html>
END_HTML_END
```

When you run that command, the sentences should appear in their
self-described time frame.

You can see that I really didn't need to do anything special to get Text-
Mate to stream this content. I did have to add the magic STDOUT.sync =
true line to prevent Ruby from buffering my output, making sure it was
sent to TextMate immediately, but TextMate showed the output as it
arrived.

One special case where output is not streamed as you might expect is
inside <pre> ... </pre> tags. Change your command body to the following code so you can see this:

automation_tips_and_tricks/pre.rb

```
#!/usr/bin/env ruby -w

STDOUT.sync = true  # flush output as we write it

puts <<END_HTML_START.strip
<html><head>
  <title>Pre Tags Don't Stream Content by Default</title>
</head><body>
  <pre>This should appeas as soon as the command starts...
END_HTML_START

sleep 1  # pause for one second

puts "This should appear one second later..."

sleep 2  # pause for two seconds

puts <<END_HTML_END
Finally, this should appear about three seconds into execution.</pre>
</body><html>
END_HTML_END
```

When you run that command, all the output should show up right at
the end of execution. However, you can make a minor change to get it
working correctly again.

Note the addition of the break tags to the ends of the preformatted text lines in the following code:

automation_tips_and_tricks/streaming_pre.rb

```
#!/usr/bin/env ruby -w

STDOUT.sync = true  # flush output as we write it

print <<END_HTML_START.strip
<html><head>
  <title>Streaming Lines in Pre Tags</title>
</head><body>
  <pre>This should appear as soon as the command starts...<br>
END_HTML_START

sleep 1  # pause for one second

print "This should appear one second later...<br>"

sleep 2  # pause for two seconds

puts <<END_HTML_END
Finally, this should appear about three seconds into execution.</pre>
</body><html>
END_HTML_END
```

I also switched to using print() instead of puts() for this code so they wouldn't have an added line end that would double the spacing. The HTML display will stream preformatted content when it runs into these break tags. Because of this, a common trick of TextMate commands is to run a substitution over output that will appear inside <br> tags to replace line endings with break tags. You can do this in Ruby with gsub("\n", "<br>").

You can use a variation of this trick when you want to stream incomplete lines. Change the code for our streaming command one last time to the following:

automation_tips_and_tricks/streaming_pre_chars.rb

```
#!/usr/bin/env ruby -w

STDOUT.sync = true  # flush output as we write it

print <<END_HTML_START.strip
<html><head>
  <title>Streaming Characters in Pre Tags</title>
</head><body>
  <pre>Loading...<br>
END_HTML_START
```

```
10.times do
  print "&gt;<br style='display: none'>"
  sleep 1  # pause for one second
end
print "<br>"

puts <<END_HTML_END
Loaded.</pre>
</body><html>
END_HTML_END
```

When you run this version, the progress indicator characters should appear one second apart, even though the line hasn't ended. You can see that I'm feeding break tags to the HTML window to keep it streaming, but the style attribute keeps them from showing up in the end result.

9.9 Building Interactive Commands

The more you work with TextMate commands, the more interactive you will want to make them. It's a natural process that makes them more flexible by allowing them to respond to your current needs. TextMate offers a couple of options for interacting with the user.

Using Dialog Boxes

The Ruby support library dialog.rb is a wrapper over the CocoaDialog application that is bundled with TextMate.[2] Using the methods provided by this library, you can display GUI dialog boxes to the user and receive their responses. Here's a list of the methods you can call on the Dialog module and the dialog boxes they display:

request_string()

Call this method to present the user with a single input field and receive their String response.

request_file()
request_files()

The singular method will present the user with a File dialog box and allow them to choose a file. The plural version is the same, but

---

2. See http://macromates.com/screencast/intro_to_tm_dialog.mov for an introduction to a different way to build dialog boxes for TextMate, using Apple's Interface Builder application. All of the Dialog methods are being converted to use this new tool, so stick to the support library and your code will be future proof.

the user is allowed to make multiple selections. You will receive the selected paths in a returned Array.

request_secure_string( )

This method presents the user with a password input box and returns the password entered.

request_item( )

This method allows the user to choose from an array of items you pass in the :itemsHash key, via a drop-down menu. The selected item is returned.

request_confirmation( )

This dialog box allows you to ask the user a simple yes/no question, often used to verify that an operation is OK. The return value will be either **true** or **false**.

All these methods accept a hash of options as their only parameter. Generally, you will want to set the dialog box :title and add some text explaining what to do with :prompt. You may also want to change the contents of :button1 and :button2. You may pass any other options supported by CocoaDialog, though. Those are described in the documentation at http://cocoadialog.sourceforge.net/documentation.html.

By default these methods return the user's answer when the OK button is clicked (:button1) and **nil** when the Cancel button (:button2) is clicked. Another way to use these methods is to pass a block to the dialog box call, in which case the code will be run if the user clicks the OK button (:button1), and the typical return value will be passed to your block instead. When a block is given, the Cancel button raises Ruby's SystemExitException, which results in a clean exit unless rescued.

You can see an example using dialog box calls in Section 8.2, *Using Ruby or Another Scripting Language*, on page 107.

Dynamic HTML

Another tool for building interactive commands is provided to those using the HTML output option. TextMate makes a TextMate object available to JavaScript code run inside HTML output. This object has an isBusy property that you can set to **true** or **false** to toggle the display of a busy wheel in the upper-right corner of the window.

The TextMate object also provides a system() method, which is similar to the method of the same name provided to Dashboard widgets. Using this method, you can run shell commands or call out to your own scripts for further processing. Here's an example command (Input: None, Output: Show as HTML) that provides a mini-shell inside TextMate's HTML output window:

`automation_tips_and_tricks/mini_shell.sh`

```
source "$TM_SUPPORT_PATH/lib/webpreview.sh"
html_header "TextMate Mini Shell" "bash"

cat <<END_SHELL
<h1>Enter shell commands below:</h1>
<pre><code id="shell"></code></pre>
<script language="JavaScript">
function run_command() {
  var s              = document.getElementById('shell');
  var com            = document.f.com.value;
  s.innerHTML        = s.innerHTML + "<b>$ " + safe(com) + "</b><br>";
  document.f.com.value = "";

        var res     = TextMate.system(com, null).outputString;
    s.innerHTML = s.innerHTML + safe(res).replace(/\n/g, "<br>");

        window.location.hash = "input_form";
}

function safe(str) {
    return str.replace(/&/g, "&amp;").replace(/</g, "&lt;").replace(/>/g, "&gt;");
}
</script>
<form id="input_form" name="f"
      onsubmit="javascript: run_command(); return false" action="#">
    <input maxlength="2048" size="55" name="com" value="">
    <input value="Run" type="submit">
</form>
END_SHELL

html_footer
```

The second argument to system() allows you to control whether the command is executed synchronously or asynchronously. Typically, Text-Mate commands will want to pass **null** for synchronous execution that waits on the command to complete. For more details on this issue, see Apple's documentation of the Dashboard equivalent.[3]

---

3. http://developer.apple.com/documentation/AppleApplications/Conceptual/Dashboard_ProgTopics/Articles/CommandLine.html

9.10 Compound Automations

Each type of TextMate automation has certain strengths. Snippets can move the caret around using tab stops. Macros can make complex selections using movement commands or regular expressions. Commands can do complex processing using a scripting language. But what if you need all three?

The good news is that TextMate automations can work together. A macro can run commands, and commands can deliver their output as snippets. Using these tools together, it's possible to make intelligent automations. Let's try one now.

In this example, we will build an automation that allows you to type a conversion statement such as "120 minutes to seconds" into TextMate that will be replaced with the result ("7,200 seconds" in this case).

The first step is to write a Ruby script for handling the conversion. That's not hard at all. Here's my offering that uses a website to do the actual conversion:

`automation_tips_and_tricks/convert.rb`

```ruby
#!/usr/bin/env ruby -w

require "open-uri"

query = ARGV.shift || STDIN.read
exit if query.nil? or query.empty?

open("http://www.convort.com/?q=#{URI.escape(query)}") do |page|
  res = page.read.scan(/<h1>\s*(\d[\d,]*(?:\.\d+)?\s+\w+)\s*<\/h1>/).last.last
  print res + "${0}"
end
```

Save that code into a file called convert.rb.

Notice that I wrote that script so it was easy to test outside TextMate. I passed it command-line arguments to make sure I had it working, but it can read from STDIN instead, which I will use to interact with TextMate. This command does return a trivial snippet, which will ensure the caret lands at the end of the result, allowing the user to keep typing.

The next step is to get this command working with TextMate. First I need to put it somewhere TextMate can see it, which in Unix terms means it needs to be in your PATH. To find your options for that, launch TextMate, run Text → Filter Through Command (⌥⌘R), and feed it the command echo "$PATH" | ruby -e 'puts ARGF.read.split(":")' with Input set to None and Output set to Show as Tool Tip. Any of the directories shown in the tooltip will work. I recommend /usr/local/bin if it's in your PATH, and you should be able to move the file there by navigating to it in the Terminal, typing sudo mv convert.rb /usr/local/bin/, and giving the system an admin password. Also make sure the file can be executed by giving the Terminal the line chmod +x /usr/local/bin/convert.rb.

You are now ready to build a macro that uses the command. With this macro, you will select the text to be converted and filter it through the command to get the desired results. It's important to note that you probably could filter the entire document through the command, make the change, and replace the document content. This is a bad idea for a couple reasons. It makes the command more complicated, and it forces TextMate to reparse the document (syntax highlighting may flash). It's better to work with just what you need instead. Here's how I built the macro:

1. Open a new TextMate document by selecting File → New, and add the example content by typing this: 120 minutes to seconds.

2. Begin macro recording by selecting Bundles → Macros → Start Recording (⌥ ⌘ M).

3. Hold down ⇧ to select as you move and ⌥ to move word by word, and then tap ← four times. That should select the amount, the from unit, the word to, and the to unit.

4. Call up Text → Filter Through Command (⌥ ⌘ R). Set the command to convert.rb, Input to Selection, and Output to Insert as Snippet. Click the Execute button. After a slight pause for the page read (you need an active internet connection for this step), you should see your converted units appear.

5. Stop macro recording by selecting Bundles → Macros → Stop Recording (⌥ ⌘ M).

You can now try your new toy. Type a few conversions, and trigger the macro for each one with Bundles → Macros → Replay Last Recording (⇧ ⌘ M). The program is pretty smart handling even abbreviations such as "50 km to miles."

If you decide you like this macro, you can save it to your Pragmatic Examples bundle as you did in Chapter 7, *Macros*, on page 91. If you do save the macro, you should move convert.rb into the bundle with it.

If you place it in the Support/bin directory of the bundle that holds the macro, the macro will be able to find it when it runs.

If you've made it this far, the hope is that you've learned features of TextMate, your Mac, and even Unix. You should definitely consider yourself a power user now. You can sure take what you've learned and start automating yourself right out of work. There's more to learn about TextMate, though, for the truly adventurous. In the next part of the book, I will explore what TextMate knows about text formats and talk about how to enhance that knowledge.

Part III

Languages

Chapter 10

Language Grammars

The languages TextMate understands are described in *grammar* files, stored in the bundles. The languages TextMate knows are just the result of the grammar files it ships with plus any you have installed or created. TextMate knows most common computer languages right out of the box. Make a new grammar describing a language, and TextMate will learn the language you describe.

Textmate recognizes elements of a language by reading the grammar for that language. Using a grammar, TextMate can color elements and manage settings and automations for the elements of that language, just as it does for all those languages it knows when you install it.

To learn how all of that works, you will teach TextMate how to recognize the structure of a new language in this chapter.

If TextMate already knows the languages you need to use it with and you are happy with how they work, you can safely skip this chapter and the next. Many users never find themselves needing to add new languages because TextMate already knows what they need.

10.1   The JSON Data Language

At the time of this writing, I'm not aware of any publicly available JSON language grammar for TextMate. I do know there have been requests for such a file, though. Let's build one.[1]

---

1. The grammar developed in this chapter was later added to the official TextMate bundles repository.

JSON is a small data exchange format, similar to YAML. It defines a minimal set of data types such as numbers and strings, plus two more complex containers: object and array. An array is an ordered sequence of elements, and an object is a collection of name and value pairs. Here are a handful of JSON construct examples:

```
true                      # a constant
42                        # a number
"JSON"                    # a string
[1, 2, "three"]           # an array of values
[1, 2, [3, 4]]            # a nested array
{"one" : 1, "false" : false}  # an object of name/value pairs
```

I added the previous comments in a fictitious syntax. JSON doesn't have comments in the language.

I'll show how to teach TextMate to break down these constructs, which leads me to the first step of building a grammar: finding some language syntax documentation. Building a grammar is all about knowing what's allowed at any given point in a language file. Do not rely on your memory. When you are building a grammar, keep the documentation handy—even for languages you know well.

JSON's syntax is explained beautifully at http://json.org/. Please take a moment to look over that document so you will better understand what you are creating here and so you will see the kind of documentation you want to hunt down when you are building a language grammar.

Creating a New Grammar

Armed with the proper knowledge, you are ready to build a grammar. Now you need to get TextMate ready! Here are the steps to prepare it:

1. Create a new TextMate document by selecting File → New (⌘ N).
2. Enter just true for the document content. This is a valid, if sparse, JSON file, and you need to start somewhere.
3. Save your new document by choosing File → Save (⌘ S), and give it a name of example.json.

This gives you a minimal JSON document to get started with. Note that TextMate still believes this document is plain text, as you can see in Figure 10.1, on the next page. It doesn't yet know what JSON is, because you haven't told it. The document is still devoid of color for this same reason. TextMate doesn't yet know how to syntax highlight it.

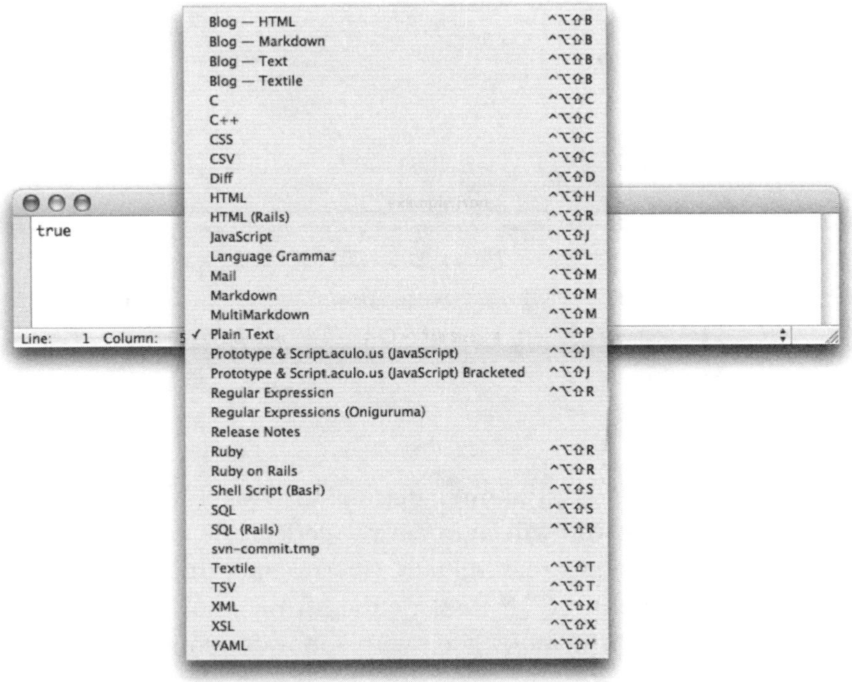

Figure 10.1: PLAIN-TEXT LANGUAGE

Here's how you create a grammar file:

1. Open the Bundle Editor by selecting Bundles → Bundle Editor → Show Bundle Editor (^ ⌥ ⌘ B).

2. Highlight your Pragmatic Examples bundle by clicking the name.

3. Create a JSON grammar by selecting New Language from the + menu in the lower-left corner of the Bundle Editor. Type JSON to name your grammar.

As you can see, TextMate gave you some boilerplate grammar syntax to help you get started. Let's set a few quick elements:

1. Change the source.untitled example scopeName to source.json, creating a unique scope for the new language. TextMate convention has you placing grammars in two top-level scopes, one for text and one for source. TextMate creator Allan Odgaard jokes that your language is text if it looks good with View → Soft Wrap (⌥ ⌘ W) activated, and everything else is source. A more scientific rule of thumb is to say that you should use source if the grammar defines a form

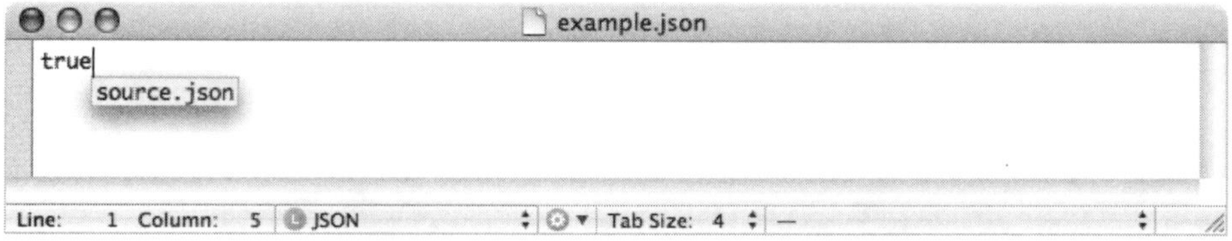

Figure 10.2: A JSON SCOPE

of quoted string and should use text if it does not. The reasoning here is that you will want source code–style handling in string constructs, such as making sure that an apostrophe isn't doubled when you type it. JSON does define strings, so it's source. Markdown does not and looks good with Soft Wrap, so it is text.

2. Between the parentheses labeled fileTypes, add a 'json' so TextMate will recognize files ending in .json as JSON files. You could list multiple options here, separated by commas, but in this case you need only one. Note that even though JSON is a legal subset of JavaScript, you would not want to add a 'js', since it could interfere with the main JavaScript grammar that comes with TextMate.

3. Finally, set Activation to Key Equivalent, and set the keystroke to ^ ⌥ ⇧ J. This is a TextMate convention, and your grammars should always use the same three modifier keys along with the first letter of the language name.

Close the Bundle Editor so TextMate will save the grammar file and put it into effect. It still needs a lot of work, but you'll get to that soon.

In your example file, use your new keystroke (^ ⌥ ⇧ J) to switch to the JSON language grammar. You will need to select JSON from the menu of J-languages TextMate pops up, if it's not the only J-language you have enabled. The language menu at the bottom of the window should now label the document correctly as JSON. Select Bundles → TextMate → Show Scope (^ ⇧ P), and TextMate will tell you that you are now inside the scope you just created. You can see these fruits of your labor in Figure 10.2.

The First Rule

With a basic grammar in place, you are ready to create *rules*. Grammars are collections of rules that divide the document syntax into scopes.

For the first rule, let's tackle the easiest element of the JSON language. JSON allows for three special constants: true, false, and null. These elements are common to almost all languages in some form, so it's useful to be able to represent them in the data language. You need to add a rule that identifies these three words.

Like so many things in TextMate, grammar rules are based on regular expressions. You should be getting pretty comfortable with regular expression syntax by now, but remember that, when in doubt, you can always refer to Section 4.2, *Mixing in Regular Expressions*, on page 42. An expression to match three words is not hard to conjure. You can use alternation to allow for the words and flank them with word boundary anchors to ensure you don't find them as part of a larger word.

The other half of the rule you need is the scope to be assigned to these words. TextMate convention is for you to use constant.language.json in this case. That may seem backward to how you would instinctually assign the scope, expecting json to be at the front. However, if you wrote scopes like that, you would need special handling for every single language TextMate knows. You would have to deal with the json scope, ruby scope, and so on. By reversing it, you can instead work with language elements that are often universal, such as a constant. If you want to add special handling for JSON constants, you can choose to target the longer scope.

Now that it's planned out, it's time to add the rule:

1. Open the Bundle Editor (^ ⌥ ⌘ B).
2. Navigate to your JSON grammar, click the language name to make it active, and place your caret inside the Edit Language: "JSON" box.
3. Use Edit in TextMate[2] to move the grammar into a regular TextMate editing window (^ ⌘ E). The editor should recognize the content and assign it the Language Grammar type, but if it doesn't, you can force the change with ^ ⌥ ⇧ L.
4. There are two example rules in the default grammar created for you by TextMate. You will see these in the patterns = (...) section,

---

2. I show how to install this tool in Section 1.4, *Installing TextMate and Tools*, on page 6.

each rule delimited by {...}. Go ahead and remove the larger second rule, but keep the first one to edit, since it's already almost exactly what you need.

5. Modify the first rule to match the words you are looking for, and assign your scope. Here's the rule I used:

language_grammars/simple_json.textmate

```
{ name = 'constant.language.json';
  match = '\b(true|false|null)\b';
},
```

6. Save (⌘ S) and close (⌘ W) the grammar document. This will update the content in the Bundle Editor.

7. You can put the new grammar into effect by closing the Bundle Editor, but TextMate provides a shortcut since grammar work is generally a lot of back and forth with the Bundle Editor. Just clicking the Test button will put your grammar into action immediately.

Don't be surprised if TextMate makes minor formatting changes to your grammar at this point or in the future. Whenever the grammar is saved, TextMate normalizes the document format.

At this point, your JSON document most likely got a splash of color! TextMate should now recognize and syntax highlight the word true. It will do more than that. Change our sample content to the following:

```
[true, false, null]
```

Notice how TextMate recognizes the words as you enter them. You can also use Show Scope (⌃ ⇧ P) to examine the scope TextMate assigns to these terms.

The brackets and commas are elements of another JSON construct not yet recognized, an array. Because these elements are not matched by a rule, they do not have scopes or styling.

Documenting a Grammar

One rule down. TextMate will now identify JSON's constants, which allows them to be syntax highlighted and targeted in automations and preferences. Let's tackle another element. This rule is more involved, so you'll need some new tricks to manage it.

The next rule you should deal with is the one to handle numbers. You want TextMate to recognize JSON's numbers and scope them appropriately, again for syntax coloring, automations, and preferences. You need to translate that syntax diagram for numbers found on the JSON documentation page and assign another TextMate standard scope.

Doing those two things, I end up with a rule that looks like this:

```
{ name = 'constant.numeric.json';
  match = '-?(?:0|[1-9]\d*)(?:\.\d+(?:[eE][+-]?\d+)?)?';
},
```

Yikes! Though it's pretty much a direct translation of the diagram, that's one ugly expression. I had to struggle my way through building it, testing it a few times along the way, and I'm sure it's no picnic for you to read. At some point, I'll probably return to this grammar to make changes, and it's almost certain I'll forget how this works by then.

The solution is a mode for regular expressions I've yet to discuss. Using the extended mode for regular expressions, you can embed whitespace and comments inside a regular expression to clarify how it functions. Inside a (?x:...) pattern, the regular expression engine ignores whitespace, and a # character turns the rest of the line it's on into a comment, which the engine also ignores.

You don't need to match whitespace in this expression, but when you do, you'll often use the \s character class shortcut anyway, so losing space characters isn't too significant. Here's how I would use extended mode to clean up the scary new rule:

`language_grammars/simple_json.textmate`

```
{ name = 'constant.numeric.json';
  comment = 'handles integer and decimal numbers';
  match = '(?x:          # turn on extended mode
            -?            # an optional minus
            (?:
              0           # a zero
              |           # ...or...
              [1-9]       # a 1-9 character
              \d*         # followed by zero or more digits
            )
            (?:
              \.          # a period
              \d+         # followed by one or more digits
              (?:
                [eE]      # an e character
                [+-]?     # followed by an option +/-
                \d+       # followed by one or more digits
              )?          # make exponent optional
            )?            # make decimal portion optional
          )';
},
```

Note that I slipped a comment element in there in addition to the expression comments. This is another helpful tool for documenting your work in grammar files.

Now, when you go to enter that rule into your growing grammar file, you can use another helpful shortcut. Language grammar files are edited in a property list file format. The syntax[3] can be slightly tedious to work with, so it's really best to let TextMate write most of it for you. You'll find snippets for this in the Bundles → TextMate → Language Grammar Snippets.

Open the grammar file in a TextMate editing window as you did before, and place your caret just after the last rule you entered. Add a comma to separate the current rule from the one you intend to add, and then type mat→ to trigger the Rule--Match snippet. The snippet will start you in the name, and you can → to the match when you are ready.

When you're done with the new rule, expand the JSON example data with some numbers so you can see TextMate pick them up:

```
[true, false, null, 10, 123.45, 0.1e-23]
```

TextMate's Language Parser

You're ready to add JSON's strings into the mix, but to get that right, I need to show you a little about how TextMate's parser works. For example, change the sample JSON content to the following:

```
"a JSON string"
```

Now, let's introduce a naive rule to match the JSON string:

```
{ name = 'string.quoted.double.json';
  match = '"[^"]*"';
},
```

I'm ignoring the escaping issues at the moment, but this rule does seem to identify the string just fine. The problem comes when you try a trickier JSON string, even without escapes. Switch the sample string to this:

```
"a
 multiline
 JSON
 string"
```

The current string rule does not match this legal JSON string. However, if you think about it, the regular expression should match. It looks for

---

3. http://developer.apple.com/documentation/Cocoa/Conceptual/PropertyLists/Articles/
OldStylePListsConcept.html#//apple_ref/doc/uid/20001012

zero or more nonquote characters surrounded by a pair of quotes, and the newlines you added are nonquote characters. Don't take my word for it, though. Open the Edit → Find → Find dialog box (⌘ F), and perform a search for the same regular expression. It will match the string.

What you're running into here is a quirk of TextMate's language parser. TextMate has to reparse a portion of the document for every single change you make in order to keep the syntax highlighting and scopes current. Now if TextMate rescanned the entire document each time you pressed a key, performance would nose-dive, and you would like the editor a lot less. To avoid that, all document parsing works one line at a time. Make sure you understood what I just said, because this is key to making TextMate grammars. You cannot write a grammar rule that works with multiple lines of content at once.

That rule does mean it's impossible to perfectly scope some language constructs with TextMate, but that's a reasonable trade-off for acceptable performance. It's also not as big a problem as you might think. I will show you the TextMate way to tame the tricky string in spite of this limitation.

Language grammars have a second kind of rule that specifies where something begins and where it ends. The beginning expression and end expression are still bound by the one-line-rule individually, but they may occur any number of lines apart. Here's a rewrite of the string rule to use the second rule type:

```
{ name = 'string.quoted.double.json';
  begin = '"';
  end = '"';
},
```

You can enter that rule with another of the grammar snippets, this one triggered with beg→ı. Enter the rule's scope; press →ı; enter the begin pattern, →ı; and finish up by entering the end pattern.

As soon as that rule is in place, TextMate will recognize the multi-line string you have been using. You're not quite finished with strings, though. You need to handle escapes. Here's one more sample string you can enter in your JSON file:

```
"a\nJSON string\nwith \"escapes\""
```

The current rule doesn't handle that too gracefully, prematurely ending the string at the first escaped quote. Another great feature of the begin/end rules is that they can specify a set of patterns matched only inside their content.[4] Even better, an element matched by one of these inner elements is consumed and thus not available as the end match. That's exactly what you need here.

Return to editing the JSON grammar, put your caret just after the semi-colon terminating the string's end pattern, press ↵, and type pat→.

Here's the pattern you need to add:

```
patterns = (
  {   name = 'constant.character.escape.json';
      match = '(?x:                 # turn on extended mode
                \\                   # a literal backslash
                (?:                  # ...followed by...
                  ["\\/bfnrt]        # one of these characters
                  |                  # ...or...
                  u                  # a u
                  [0-9a-fA-F]{4}     # and four hex digits
                )
              )';
  }
);
```

The addition of that rule will have TextMate parsing any legal JSON string you care to throw at it. However, it is good grammar etiquette to scope the string delimiters in case automations need to identify them. Let's add that.

When you enter an expression for a grammar rule, you can make captures inside that expression normally. You can then use another feature of rules to assign scopes to just those captures. Here are the additions for the string rule:

```
beginCaptures = { 0 = {
  name = 'punctuation.definition.string.begin.json'; }; };
endCaptures = { 0 = {
  name = 'punctuation.definition.string.end.json'; }; };
```

As you can see, you can specify scopes for beginCaptures and endCaptures separately. You identify capture groups by numbers, just as you would with the replacement variables of the Find dialog box. In this case, though, since you want to scope the entire match, you can save yourself the trouble of adding parentheses to set 1 and just use the 0 shortcut to scope the entire match.

---

4. In fact, you must nest patterns to match anything inside a begin/end rule. Outer rules do not match inside these rules.

For a quick final touch, you can drop in another escaping rule to help catch typos. This isn't strictly needed, but users of the JSON grammar will benefit when the syntax highlighting calls out their mistakes immediately. Since the earlier rule covered all legal escapes, slotting this catchall beneath it handles everything else that looks like an escape:

```
{   name = 'invalid.illegal.unrecognized-string-escape.json';
    match = '\\.';
}
```

For reference, the complete rule for JSON strings is as follows:

language_grammars/simple_json.textmate

```
  { name = 'string.quoted.double.json';
    begin = '"';
    end = '"';
    beginCaptures = { 0 = {
      name = 'punctuation.definition.string.begin.json'; }; };
    endCaptures = { 0 = {
      name = 'punctuation.definition.string.end.json'; }; };
    patterns = (
      { name = 'constant.character.escape.json';
        match = '(?x:                      # turn on extended mode
                    \\                      # a literal backslash
                    (?:                     # ...followed by...
                       ["\\/bfnrt]          # one of these characters
                       |                    # ...or...
                       u                    # a u
                       [0-9a-fA-F]{4}       # and four hex digits
                    )
                  )';
      },
      { name = 'invalid.illegal.unrecognized-string-escape.json';
        match = '\\.';
      },
    );
  },
);
```

The Pattern Repository

You're doing well with the basic JSON language elements. Now you need to focus on the array and object constructs, which can contain other language elements. When grammars get recursive, the pattern *repository* is a great tool for keeping things straight.

TextMate grammars can have a pattern repository, which is just a collection of named patterns. At any point in the grammar, you may refer to the patterns in the repository by name.

The idea here is that arrays can contain all the elements you have already built, and you definitely don't want to duplicate all that work. Instead, you can move your patterns out of the patterns section and into the repository assigning names for them as you do. Here's a start for the repository definition, which you can enter with the rep→ snippet:

```
repository =
{ constant = { };
  number = { };
  string = { };
};
```

Add that just after the top-level patterns definition in your grammar. Now you want to move your rules inside those blank definitions. For example, constant should end up looking like this:

`language_grammars/json.textmate`

```
constant = {
  name = 'constant.language.json';
  match = '\b(?:true|false|null)\b';
};
```

Individual rules are great, but you really want to group them into a single element as the JSON documentation does. The documentation uses the term *value* so I will too, for clarity. The value definition needs to wrap the previous elements, and you can accomplish that with the include property for language grammars. Break in the inc→ snippet to build up this new definition for the repository:

```
value =
{ comment = "the 'value' diagram at http://json.org";
  patterns = (
    { include = '#constant'; },
    { include = '#number'; },
    { include = '#string'; },
  );
};
```

You can use the include directive to access a few different elements. When you want a repository definition, as shown here, you just use the name of the definition preceded by a number sign. Now you have a single definition that includes all three of the previous rules.

That leads to the question of what to do with the chopped-up patterns section for the grammar itself. Well, I'm happy to report that it can get a whole lot smaller, thanks to the repository:

```
patterns = ( { include = '#value'; } );
```

That completes you reorganization effort, and your JSON grammar should be back to working order if you want to check it. You didn't add any functionality this time, but you set things up good for arrays and objects.

Nested Rules

With the repository populated, a rule to isolate arrays isn't too different from the rule you built for strings. You can use a begin/end rule based on the enclosing brackets. Here's the new rule to add to the repository:

```
array =
  { name = 'meta.structure.array.json';
    begin = '\[';
    end = '\]';
    beginCaptures = { 0 = {
      name = 'punctuation.definition.array.begin.json'; }; };
    endCaptures = { 0 = {
      name = 'punctuation.definition.array.end.json'; }; };
  };
```

The meta scope used here is the TextMate convention for marking up larger portions of a document. These scopes aren't generally styled but are commonly used in limiting the scope of automations.

The patterns contained within an array aren't much more work. The value definition takes care of the majority of the legal values, and then you just need a rule for the comma separator. After spending this whole chapter bouncing back and forth between the similar JSON and property list documents, though, I was making some silly mistakes and decided to add a rule to help catch them. Here's the pattern list I used:

```
patterns = (
  { include = '#value'; },
  { name = 'punctuation.separator.array.json';
    match = ',';
  },
  { name = 'invalid.illegal.expected-array-separator.json';
    match = '[^\s\]]';
  },
);
```

Don't let that invalid rule fool you into thinking this is a strict grammar. The invalid rule still won't catch plenty of mistakes, such as multiple

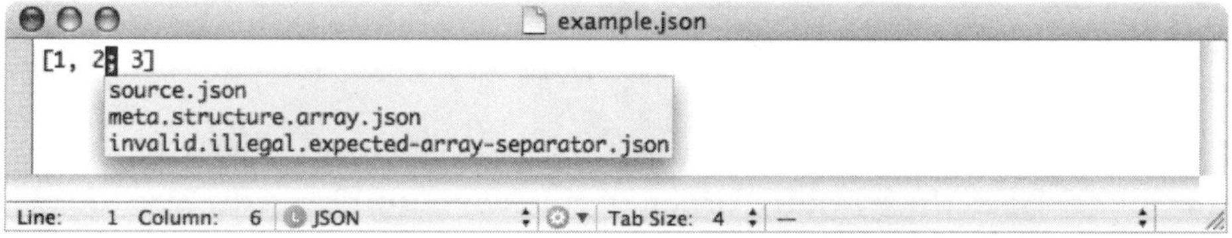

Figure 10.3: SEPARATOR TYPO FLAGGED ILLEGAL

commas without a value between them. It does flag some simple errors, though, like the one shown in Figure 10.3.

Note that I embedded a description of the error flagged in the scope that matched it. This could be useful to automations that report or even try to correct errors. You may also want to style some errors differently, so it's nice to be able to target the specific cases. You need to add one more line to the value definition patterns to kick-start the array rule:

`language_grammars/json.textmate`

```
{  include = '#array'; },
```

Try the definition by changing the JSON content to something like this:

```
[1, "a \"JSON\" sting", null, [4, true, "another string"]]
```

TextMate will pick up on the recursive definition here, since the grammar allows it. You can see how the scopes nest in Figure 10.4.

Peeking at the Document

Supporting the JSON object type is similar to the array rule you just created, but it requires one more technique that comes up regularly in building grammars. The basic repository definition for objects is similar to the definition for arrays:

```
object =
{ name = 'meta.structure.dictionary.json';
  comment = 'a JSON object';
  begin = '\{';
  end = '\}';
  beginCaptures = { 0 = {
    name = 'punctuation.definition.dictionary.begin.json'; }; };
  endCaptures = { 0 = {
    name = 'punctuation.definition.dictionary.end.json'; }; };
  patterns = ( );
};
```

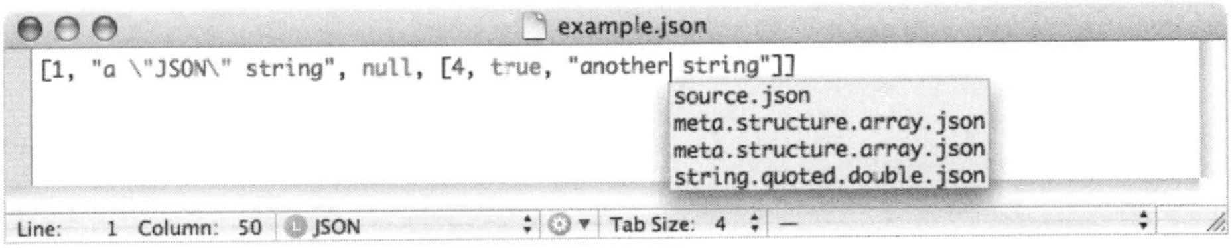

Figure 10.4: NESTED SCOPES

The surprising change in the previous code is that I have elected to scope the type as a dictionary even though the JSON documentation refers to the type as an *object*. This associative array structure of key/value pairs is common in many programming languages, often called a *hash*, *hashtable*, *dictionary*, or *map*. In TextMate grammars, it makes sense to standardize the scopes so you can work with this construct the same way in any language. The property list grammar calls it a dictionary, so I felt it best to reuse that term here.

The only task that remains is to specify the patterns for the object. The first just needs to cover object keys, and you've handled that kind of include before:

`language_grammars/json.textmate`

```
{ comment = 'the JSON object key';
  include = '#string';
},
```

The second rule is the challenge. You need a rule to represent object values. As a reminder, JSON objects have a form like this:

```
{"one" : 1, "two" : 2, "Three": 3}
```

Notice how each of the values has a leading colon. That is a hint that you could use that as a begin pattern. What would you use for the end pattern, though? Most values end with a trailing comma, but the last one does not. Now, you will know you are at the last key if you can see the brace that ends the object. You have to be careful not to consume that brace, though, since the end rule for object still needs to match it.

The solution is to peek ahead for the brace using the look-ahead feature of TextMate's regular expression engine. That allows you to confirm that there is a brace coming but leave in the content to be matched by the end pattern for object. Here's how that rule comes together:

```
language_grammars/json.textmate
{   name = 'meta.structure.dictionary.value.json';
    begin = ':';
    end = '(,)|(?=\})';
    beginCaptures = { 0 = {
      name = 'punctuation.separator.dictionary.key-value.json'; }; };
    endCaptures = { 1 = {
      name = 'punctuation.separator.dictionary.pair.json'; }; };
    patterns = (
      {   comment = 'the JSON object value';
          include = '#value';
      },

      {   name = 'invalid.illegal.expected-dictionary-separator.json';
          match = '[^\s,]';
      },
    );
},
```

The fancy end pattern is the tricky piece of this puzzle. It looks for a comma, which it can safely consume, or peeks ahead for the closing brace. Note that the comma is captured in group 1 when present and assigned a scope by endCaptures. Again, using the look-arounds as shown here is one of the secrets to grammar mastery, so make sure you understand this rule before continuing.

Let's add one more rule to catch some invalid input, as you did with array:

```
language_grammars/json.textmate
{   name = 'invalid.illegal.expected-dictionary-separator.json';
    match = '[^\s\}]';
},
```

Finally, you need to insert object into the value definition:

```
language_grammars/json.textmate
{   include = '#object'; },
```

Folding Markers

I have ignored two top-level grammar elements through this entire discussion: foldingStartMarker and foldingStopMarker. TextMate uses these two expressions to decide where to place folding markers in the gutter. The user can use these markers to collapse sections of code, as discussed in Section 3.1, *Folding Sections of Code*, on page 24.

Joe Asks...

How Strict Should My Grammar Be?

Remember the goals of a grammar: to provide syntax highlighting, to control where some settings are active, and to restrict where certain automations function. Syntax highlighting is an aid to users and it can certainly be of value to catch errors, but the goal does not need to be a perfectly accurate language definition.

For example, in a language such as Java the signature of a method looks like this:

```
public static void main(String[] args) { }
```

However, if you write a rule targeting the entire signature, users will need to do a lot of typing before they get any feedback from the syntax highlighting. It would be much better to address terms such as public, static, and void individually so TextMate can recognize them as soon as they are entered. This may allow some illegal combinations, but it's more likely to help the user catch simple typos.

On the other hand, if you're going to write a rule to catch similar identifiers, such as NSString, NSData, NSArray, and NSDictionary, you should prefer a more specific rule. The expression '\bNS(?:String|Data|Array|Dictionary)\b' will catch more errors than '\bNS[A-Z][a-z]+\b'.

Don't forget to consider the kind of language the grammar is for as well. A grammar for a free-form markup language such as Markdown doesn't need to be very strict, but the grammar for a data language such as the one we keep using to edit property lists needs to be a bit strict to catch more editing errors. The truth is that the JSON grammar in this chapter is probably a bit too forgiving, but making it strict complicates the example beyond the scope of this book.

Building good folding marker expressions is a work of art, but the basic premise is to construct a start expression to match on any line you would like to begin a fold and construct a stop expression that matches lines where the fold would end. The usual one-line-at-a-time limitation of TextMate's parser applies, and you have to consider another issue.

TextMate matches the start and stop markers based on indention level, which must be the same for both. This heuristic works for the majority of cases and is nothing you have any control over, but just keep that in mind as you build and test folding expressions.

This is another great place to use regular expression comments to document your thinking. Here are the folding expressions I came up with while playing with examples at http://www.json.org/example.html:

language_grammars/json.textmate

```
foldingStartMarker = '(?x:      # turn on extended mode
                      ^         # a line beginning with
                      \s*       # some optional space
                      [{\[]     # the start of an object or array
                      (?!       # but not followed by
                        .*      # whatever
                        [}\]]   # and the close of an object or array
                        ,?      # an optional comma
                        \s*     # some optional space
                        $       # at the end of the line
                      )
                      |         # ...or...
                      [{\[]     # the start of an object or array
                      \s*       # some optional space
                      $         # at the end of the line
                    )';
foldingStopMarker = '(?x:      # turn on extended mode
                      ^         # a line beginning with
                      \s*       # some optional space
                      [}\]]     # and the close of an object or array
                    )';
```

Probably the best tip I can give you for getting the hang of building good folding markers is to look over the grammars that ship with TextMate. You can usually find a language similar to your own and adapt the expressions to fit. I used the property list expressions as the basis for these JSON equivalents, for example.

The Complete Grammar

Putting everything together, you have built a complete and ready-to-use JSON grammar. Here's the complete example grammar:

```
language_grammars/json_full.textmate
```

```
{ scopeName = 'source.json';
  fileTypes = ( 'json' );
  foldingStartMarker = '(?x:      # turn on extended mode
                        ^         # a line beginning with
                        \s*       # some optional space
                        [{\[]     # the start of an object or array
                        (?!       # but not followed by
                          .*      # whatever
                          [}\]]   # and the close of an object or array
                          ,?      # an optional comma
                          \s*     # some optional space
                          $       # at the end of the line
                        )
                        |         # ...or...
                        [{\[]     # the start of an object or array
                        \s*       # some optional space
                        $         # at the end of the line
                      )';
  foldingStopMarker = '(?x:    # turn on extended mode
                        ^       # a line beginning with
                        \s*     # some optional space
                        [}\]]   # and the close of an object or array
                      )';
  patterns = ( { include = '#value'; } );
  repository = {
    array = {
      name = 'meta.structure.array.json';
      begin = '\[';
      end = '\]';
      beginCaptures = { 0 = {
        name = 'punctuation.definition.array.begin.json'; }; };
      endCaptures = { 0 = {
        name = 'punctuation.definition.array.end.json'; }; };
      patterns = (
        { include = '#value'; },
        { name = 'punctuation.separator.array.json';
          match = ',';
        },
        { name = 'invalid.illegal.expected-array-separator.json';
          match = '[^\s\]]';
        },
      );
    };
```

```
constant = {
  name = 'constant.language.json';
  match = '\b(?:true|false|null)\b';
};
number = {
  name = 'constant.numeric.json';
  comment = 'handles integer and decimal numbers';
  match = '(?x:         # turn on extended mode
            -?          # an optional minus
            (?:
              0         # a zero
              |         # ...or...
              [1-9]     # a 1-9 character
              \d*       # followed by zero or more digits
            )
            (?:
              \.        # a period
              \d+       # followed by one or more digits
              (?:
                [eE]    # an e character
                [+-]?   # followed by an option +/-
                \d+     # followed by one or more digits
              )?        # make exponent optional
            )?          # make decimal portion optional
          )';
};
object = {
  name = 'meta.structure.dictionary.json';
  comment = 'a JSON object';
  begin = '\{';
  end = '\}';
  beginCaptures = { 0 = {
    name = 'punctuation.definition.dictionary.begin.json'; }; };
  endCaptures = { 0 = {
    name = 'punctuation.definition.dictionary.end.json'; }; };
  patterns = (
    { comment = 'the JSON object key';
      include = '#string';
    },
    { name = 'meta.structure.dictionary.value.json';
      begin = ':';
      end = '(,)|(?=\})';
      beginCaptures = { 0 = {
        name = 'punctuation.separator.dictionary.key-value.json'; }; };
      endCaptures = { 1 = {
        name = 'punctuation.separator.dictionary.pair.json'; }; };
      patterns = (
        { comment = 'the JSON object value';
          include = '#value';
        },
```

```
                { name = 'invalid.illegal.expected-dictionary-separator.json';
                  match = '[^\s,]';
                },
              );
          },
          { name = 'invalid.illegal.expected-dictionary-separator.json';
            match = '[^\s\}]';
          },
        );
      };
    string = {
      name = 'string.quoted.double.json';
      begin = '"';
      end = '"';
      beginCaptures = { 0 = {
        name = 'punctuation.definition.string.begin.json'; }; };
      endCaptures = { 0 = {
        name = 'punctuation.definition.string.end.json'; }; };
      patterns = (
        { name = 'constant.character.escape.json';
          match = '(?x:                    # turn on extended mode
                   \\                       # a literal backslash
                   (?:                      # ...followed by...
                   ["\\/bfnrt]              # one of these characters
                   |                        # ...or...
                   u                        # a u
                   [0-9a-fA-F]{4}           # and four hex digits
                   )
                 )';
        },
        { name = 'invalid.illegal.unrecognized-string-escape.json';
          match = '\\.';
        },
      );
    };
    value = {
      comment = "the 'value' diagram at http://json.org";
      patterns = (
        { include = '#constant'; },
        { include = '#number'; },
        { include = '#string'; },
        { include = '#array'; },
        { include = '#object'; },
      );
    };
  };
}
```

10.2 Language Grammar Reference

You may choose to define six top-level language elements for your grammar files. The following is a brief description of the purpose of each key:

scopeName

> This is the overall scope assigned to the entire file when this grammar is in effect. As I explained in Section 10.1, *Creating a New Grammar*, on page 142, the grammar should begin with text or source. It's also important to note that you should extend the scopes for specializations of an existing language so all the automations, settings, and syntax coloring for the existing language extend to the specialization. For example, a proprietary XML format would be scoped text.xml.proprietary-format-name.

fileTypes

> This is a list of file extensions for which this grammar should be in effect. The user can override these rules, but by default this is how TextMate determines the language for an opened document.

firstLineMatch

> An alternate means of establishing a file's language, this regular expression is matched against the first line of the document when it is opened. If it matches, this grammar will be assigned for the document. This is commonly used to recognize Unix shebang lines.

foldingStartMarker
foldingStopMarker

> As covered in Section 10.1, *Folding Markers*, on page 156, these expressions help TextMate locate sections of code that can be folded by the user.

patterns

> This is the list of rules used to parse the document content. See Section 10.2, *Rule Reference*, on the next page, for an explanation of the individual rule elements.

repository

> This is an association of named rules usable throughout the grammar. The keys are the names for the individual rules, with the associated value being the rule itself.

Rule Reference

The rules of a language grammar have their own keys with unique meaning in the context of the rule definitions. The following is a list of the keys available with descriptions of their usage:

name

> This is the name of the scope applied to content matched by this rule. This scope should follow the TextMate conventions detailed in Section 10.2, *Scope Reference*, on the following page.

match

> This is the regular expression matching the portion of content that should be assigned this rule's scope. A rule should contain this key or begin and end keys, but not both.

begin
end

> These are a pair of expressions marking where a rule starts and stops. A rule should contain both of these keys or the match key.

> You can access captured portions of the begin expression in the end expression using back references. For example, the following rule matches a do...end pair such as a block in Ruby, but only if they have the same indent level:

```
{ name = 'meta.syntax.indented-block';
  begin = '^(\s*).*\bdo\b\s*$';
  end = '^\1end';
},
```

patterns

> This is a list of subrules matched only between begin and end patterns.

include

> This key references the current grammar, other grammars, or rules in the repository. To nest the current grammar in a rule, use this:

```
{ include = '$self'; }
```

> A grammar nested inside other grammars may nest the current top-level grammar with the following:

```
{ include = '$base'; }
```

> You can also reference any currently loaded grammar file by name:

```
{ include = 'source.json'; }
```

Finally, you can use this directive to reference patterns from the repository of this grammar:

```
{ include = '#array'; }
```

applyEndPatternLast

If an end expression and a nested rule from patterns will match at the same character, the end pattern usually gets first crack at the content. This directive swaps the regular order, giving the nested rule first shot at the match.

contentName

When provided, this scope name is assigned to all content between the begin and end patterns.

captures
beginCaptures
endCaptures

These are key/value pairs used to assign scopes to captured portions of the rule expressions. The key is the match variable number you want to scope the contents of, and the value is an attribute list with a scope in a name key. Use captures to target groups from match or as a shortcut to assign the same scope to captures in begin and end patterns. Alternately, you can target just beginCaptures and/or endCaptures:

```
{ name = 'variable.other.readwrite.class.ruby';
  match = '(@@)(\w+)';
  captures = {
    1 = { name = 'punctuation.definition.variable.class.ruby'; };
    2 = { name = 'variable.other.readwrite.class.name.ruby'; };
  };
},
```

disabled

This switch is a tool for solving problems in language grammars. Just set disabled to 1 to shut off a rule. This can be handy for isolating issues in the grammar. When you have the problem worked out, just delete the disabled setting to restore the rule.

Scope Reference

TextMate does not enforce any scope-naming rules on you as a grammar creator. However, a set of conventions has formed in the Text-Mate community to keep new grammars in line with current practices. Observing these conventions allows you to design intelligent commands that work for multiple language and ensures that your languages will work with existing themes. These are the scopes your grammars should use:

comment

This scope is for comments embedded in your language. Subtypes divide comments by type:

comment.line.double-slash
comment.line.number-sign
comment.line.*

> The comment.line subtype is for single-line comments in a language. You should always append a description of the comment character so it can be extracted from the scope by commands.

comment.block

> This scope is for multiline comments.

comment.block.documentation

> Use this to identify embedded documentation such as Java's Java-Doc comments.

constant

A namespace for the unchanging elements of a language. Here's the list by subtype:

constant.numeric

> Constants that represent numbers: 42, 1.5, 0xFF.

constant.character

> Constants that represent characters, such as HTML's <.

constant.character.escape

> Escaped characters, commonly found in the strings of programming languages. Examples include \t. \n, and \141.

constant.language

> Constants provided by the language: true, false, nil.

constant.other

> Any constant not covered by the previous categories, such as colors in CSS.

entity

This scope involves the larger sections of a document: a chapter, a class, or a tag. Although the entire section will be scoped as a meta subtype, the entity scope is used for the names and titles of a section.

entity.name.function

> The name of a function

entity.name.type.class
entity.name.type.module
entity.name.type.*

> The name of a type declaration, such as a class or module

entity.name.tag

> The name of a tag in a markup language

entity.name.section

> The name of a section or heading

entity.other.inherited-class

> The name of a parent class used in the definition of a child class

entity.other.attribute-name

> The name of an attribute for a tag

invalid

You should use this scope to flag elements of a language that are malformed or outdated.

invalid.illegal

> An illegal piece of syntax, such as a bare & in an XML document.

invalid.deprecated

> Use this scope to flag old APIs that should no longer be used.

keyword

You can place keywords not covered by other scopes here. Subtypes are as follows:

keyword.control

> Keywords used in flow control: if, for, return

keyword.operator

> For operators that have a textual representation, such as or

keyword.other

> All other keywords

punctuation

This is a new categorization for the operators of a language. In addition to using the following subtypes, you can tack on a trailing .begin or .end for paired operators, before the language identifier at the end of the scope:

punctuation.definition
> The scope for punctuation used to delimit single objects: an array, a string, a header, a list, a table

punctuation.section
> The scope for punctuation used to delimit a structured section: a comment, a function, a scope, a quote, a paragraph

punctuation.separator
> The scope for punctuation used to separate elements of content: key/value pairs or arguments

punctuation.terminator
> The scope for punctuation used to terminate an element: a statement, a rule, a line

markup

The scope for elements used to mark up text. Categories reflect the constructs offered by markup popular markup languages:

markup.underline
> Text that should be underlined.

markup.underline.link
> For external references. Typically URLs.
>
> Links are nested under markup.underline as a convenience for themes. If no link styling is specified, they will inherit the fairly standard convention of being underlined.

markup.bold
> For text that should be bold or strongly emphasized.

markup.italic
> For text that should be italic or emphasized.

markup.heading
> For section titles. You can append a nesting level, as in markup.heading.2.html for HTML.

list.numbered
list.unnumbered
list.*
> For textual lists, by type.

markup.quote
> Quoted, or block-quoted, text.

markup.raw
> For text that should be rendered verbatim, such as code listings. Spell checking is generally disabled in these sections.

markup.other
> For all other markup constructs.

meta

This scope is for marking up larger portions of a document, such as functions or data structure definitions. The scope is not usually styled, but you can use it to limit the reach of automations.

storage

For types and modifiers:

storage.type
> Used to scope storage type identifiers: class, function, int

storage.modifier
> The scope for storage modifier identifiers: abstract, final, static

string

Used to mark up a run of character data in most languages. Subtypes divide string and near-string types:

string.quoted.single
string.quoted.double
string.quoted.triple
string.quoted.other
> For quoted strings, by kind of quote used. Triple-quoted strings are used in Python, and string.quoted.other is for other kinds of quoting, such as $'shell' or %q{}.

string.unquoted
> For here-docs and here-strings.

string.interpolated
> For evaluated strings, such as `date` or $(pwd).

string.regexp
>   For regular expression literals.

string.other
>   For all other string types.

support

This scope address language elements provided by frameworks and libraries. The categories are as follows:

support.function
>   For functions provided by frameworks and libraries

support.class
>   For classes provided by frameworks and libraries

support.type
>   For types provided by frameworks and libraries, such as C's type-defs and structs

support.constant
>   For constants provided by frameworks and libraries

support.variable
>   For variables provided by frameworks and libraries

support.other
>   For any other constructs provided by frameworks and libraries

variable

The scope covering user variable entities. The three types are as follows:

variable.parameter
>   Used to scope function parameter variables

variable.language
>   Used to scope reserved variables, such as this or self

variable.other
>   Used to scope all other variables

It's more important to spread your language elements out among the listed scopes than to perfectly model your language's syntax. If you lump everything under the keyword scope, your entire language will be syntax highlighted identically, no matter how true to the syntax you are being. Also, remember to reuse scope subtypes and work from general to specific, always slotting the language name on the far right.

TextMate ships with a tool you can use to validate the scopes in your newly created bundle. The script reads syntax files and then prints the names of any scopes not matching the conventions. You can run the check by feeding the Terminal:

```
ruby \
/Applications/TextMate.app/Contents/SharedSupport/Support/bin/validate_bundle.rb \
/path/to/your/bundle
```

Building new grammars isn't for everyone and not often needed, but a rare few of us actually find it fun to twiddle and tweak TextMate's core. You should now know whether you are one of us. Even if you're not, you can use this knowledge to make changes to TextMate's editing behaviors and syntax highlighting. I'll talk about that next.

Chapter 11

Preferences and Themes

Once a language grammar exists, you are free to use the scopes it assigns to the contents of your documents. This helps improve your work environment by customizing TextMate to respond to the way you think. I talked about how you can and should use scopes to limit the reach of automations in Section 6.2, *Limiting Snippet Scope*, on page 88, but you can use other ways to make TextMate change behavior depending on the content you are currently editing.

You can use scopes to change two aspects for documents that contain them. The changes you don't generally see are called *preferences*, and they subtly shift TextMate's behavior to make your editing jobs that much easier. The obvious changes occur in syntax highlight coloring and styles that are managed by *themes*. This chapter covers how to modify both of these elements.

11.1 Preferences

You should already be familiar with TextMate → Preferences (⌘ ,), which you can use to set global TextMate functionality. That's not what I am discussing in this chapter. The preferences you create here will be more tightly focused, altering functionality only at certain places in a certain kind of document.

Altering a preference will cause TextMate to subtly adjust certain behaviors of the editor in the areas you indicate. Given that, a preference always involves two specifications. The first is a description of the setting you would like to adjust. These descriptions are written in the same property list format you used to create a grammar file in Chapter 10,

Language Grammars, on page 141. The second specification for a preference is where you would like the change to take effect. This is just a list of scopes, just as you would apply for limiting an automation.

Setting a preference is similar to making a small grammar file. Here's the process:

1. Open the Bundle Editor by selecting Bundles → Bundle Editor → Show Bundle Editor (^ ⌥ ⌘ B).

2. Highlight the name of the bundle to which you want to add a preference. Preference files are usually stored in the same bundle as the grammar file whose scopes they affect, but this is not a requirement.

3. Create a preference file by selecting New Preferences from the + menu in the lower-left corner of the Bundle Editor. Type a name for your file, which is traditionally the setting it changes: Spell Checking, Symbol List, and so on.

4. Enter the settings (from the following sections of this chapter) you would like to change between the empty braces TextMate provides you.

5. Provide a scope selector that limits the setting change to content inside the scope or scopes you want to alter. I discuss this process in Section 6.2, *Limiting Snippet Scope*, on page 88.

The following sections highlight the preferences currently used by TextMate. I will cover the changes you can make to these settings and how they will affect TextMate behavior.

Spell Checking

This setting makes TextMate's spelling checker super smart, and it's just a single switch you can flip on and off as needed. By default, the spelling checker will validate every word in the document, but that's not always what you want. Programming and markup languages often have nonsensical identifiers such as fileno() and DOCTYPE. You don't want to see squiggly red lines under terms like that. Because of that, the Source bundle contains this trivial preference file:

```
{ spellChecking = 0; }
```

As you probably guessed, the 0 setting disables spell checking. In contrast, you could use 1 to reenable checking.

That file has a scope selector of source, constant, keyword, storage, support, variable, which covers all the conventional scopes used for the elements of programming languages. However, even that rule isn't perfect. Programs commonly contain strings filled with human-readable content, and you should spell check that. That's why the Source bundle contains a second spelling preference file scoped to source string.quoted with these contents:

```
{ spellChecking = 1; }
```

This setting restores spell-checking functionality to quoted strings located inside the source scope that the last file disabled. You can use this same setting to ensure the proper parts of your documents are spell checked.

Paired Characters

Two different settings fall under this category but are closely related:

smartTypingPairs

A list of two character lists. When the first character of any list is inserted in the indicated scope, TextMate immediately adds the second character behind the caret, as described in Section 3.3, *Inserting New Content*, on page 28.

highlightPairs

A list of two character lists. When the caret is moved over any of the second characters in these lists, TextMate will highlight the matching first character of the list for a short time. This helps the user identify the nesting of these paired characters.

The Text bundle sets the following pairs in an unscoped file, which will make them available anywhere that doesn't override the settings:

```
{ highlightPairs = (
    ( '(', ')' ),
    ( '{', '}' ),
    ( '[', ']' ),
    ( '“', '”' ),
    ( '‘', '’' ),
  );
  smartTypingPairs = (
    ( '"', '"' ),
    ( '(', ')' ),
    ( '{', '}' ),
    ( '[', ']' ),
    ( '“', '”' ),
    ( '‘', '’' ),
  );
}
```

Notice the lack of a ("″", "″") smart typing pair. That character is commonly typed as an apostrophe and will likely annoy you in pairs. However, the Source bundle overrides this setting for most places of a source code file, where it is commonly used to delimit strings.

Symbol List

TextMate maintains a list of *symbols* in the current document. These are hotspots in the content you can return to as needed, as discussed in Section 3.1, *Moving to a Line, Symbol, or Bookmark*, on page 23. This preference controls how that list gets populated, and it consists of two directives:

showInSymbolList

> Set this directive to 1 to have the contents of the indicated scope added to the symbol list.

symbolTransformation

> This is a collection of one or more regular expressions used to transform all symbol list entries before they are added to the list. Expressions should have the form s/match-exp/replacement/ options, and you separate multiple patterns with semicolons. You are allowed to add comments to this mini-program using the number sign.

For example, the Markdown bundle includes a preference file scoped to text.html.markdown markup.heading.markdown with the following contents:

```
{ showInSymbolList = 1;
  symbolTransformation = "
    s/\s*#*\s*\z//g;              # strip trailing space and #'s
    s/(?<=#)#/ /g;          # change all but first # to m-space
    s/^#( *)\s+(.*)/$1$2/;  # strip first # and space before title
  ";
}
```

This ensures that Markdown headers of the form ### My Header ### are added to the symbol list. Before they are placed there, three regular expressions remove unneeded formatting characters. The /g option means "global" and causes TextMate to repeat the match until it fails. That's the only option you will ever need to add.

Indentation

When you type an else or an end in a Ruby document, TextMate reduces the indent of that line one level so it will line up with the correspond-

ing if or while. It knows to make these changes thanks to the following
settings:

increaseIndentPattern

This is a regular expression indicating lines that increase the indent pattern. TextMate will increase the indent one level starting
on the line following the match and continue with the new indention level until you manually change the indent or until it matches
another pattern.

Many programming languages use braces to wrap sections of code,
so a common pattern for this setting is a variation of the following
trivial code:

```
increaseIndentPattern = '\{';
```

The actual patterns can be considerably more complex since they
need to account for issues such as comments and the closing
brace possibly being on the same line. Take a peek at the C bundle's rules for a moderate example.

decreaseIndentPattern

This is a regular expression signaling the end of a series of indented lines. TextMate decreases the indent level on the matched line
and for all the lines following it.

Again, this is commonly some variation of a closing brace pattern:

```
decreaseIndentPattern = '\}';
```

indentNextLinePattern

This pattern functions exactly like increaseIndentPattern, except it
affects only the line immediately following the matched pattern.

Some languages, such as C and Java, allow conditional constructs
that affect only the following statement. For example:

```
if (...)
    ...;
```

These constructs are common targets for indentNextLinePattern.

unIndentedLinePattern

Some lines occur outside the regular document indention and
should, in fact, not even affect the current level of indent. You
can specify a regular expression in this directive to match lines
for TextMate to ignore.

C preprocessor statements are an ideal target for unIndentedLine-
Pattern, because they break the regular document flow:

```
   ...
#if ...
   ...
#endif
   ...
```

Shell Variables

In addition to setting environment variables and project-level variables,
as described in more detail in Section 9.2, *TextMate's Environment Variables*, on page 113, you can set variables that are active only when you
are in certain scopes. This makes automations that use these variables
context-sensitive, since the information they read from the variables
will change depending on where the user is.

Bundles → Source → Comment Line/Selection (⌘ /) uses this feature to read
comment markers for the current language. When you add new bundles to TextMate, you need only to provide a preference file that sets
the comment variables for that language, and the command will work
with the new creation. Here's that file from the Ruby bundle, scoped to
source.ruby:

```
{ shellVariables = (
    { name = 'TM_COMMENT_START';
      value = '# ';
    },
    { name = 'TM_COMMENT_START_2';
      value = '=begin
';
    },
    { name = 'TM_COMMENT_END_2';
      value = '=end
';
    },
  );
}
```

Setting variables is a simple matter of assigning to the shellVariables
directive a list of name/value pairs. The name is the variable to set, and
the value is the string content placed in the variable.

This is just one example of variables supported by TextMate out of the
box. Feel free to set your own unique shellVariables and to take advantage
of them in your own automations.

Completions

I recommended you start wearing out the ↺ key for completions all the way back in Section 3.3, *Inserting New Content*, on page 28. By default, that command builds a word list for the matches based on current document content. You can customize that with the following settings, though:

completions

> This list of words will be added to the words matched from the document when a completion is triggered. You can use this to insert language keywords or common API calls so a user does not need to type the term before it can be matched.

disableDefaultCompletion

> Set this directive to 1 to shut off the regular completion behavior of adding document matched words to the list.

completionCommand

> This super override allows you to provide a shell command to handle completions in any custom manner you choose. Your script can access the word for completion in the TM_CURRENT_WORD environment variable and should return a list of possible completions, one per line.

> The Ruby bundle has a nice example of this in action, with the following command scoped to meta.require.ruby string.quoted:

```
{ completionCommand = '#!/usr/bin/env ruby
    ptrn = /^#{Regexp.escape ENV["TM_CURRENT_WORD"].to_s}[^.]+\..+/
    puts( $LOAD_PATH.inject([]) do |res, path|
      res + Dir.new(path).grep(ptrn) { |file| file[/^[^.]+/] }
    end.sort.uniq )'; }
```

> The scope limits this command to being triggered when a completion is attempted inside a Ruby require string. It returns a list of files in the load path matching the current word. This allows you to type req→ followed by str↺ to require "stringio".

11.2 Themes

Once a grammar file has divided a document into scopes, TextMate can syntax highlight the various elements. Your current theme handles the decision of which color to make each element.

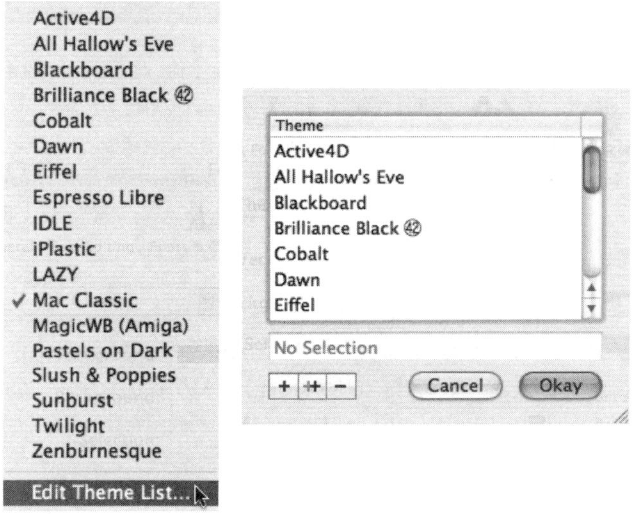

Figure 11.1: THEME LIST SHEET

To view your current theme or change to a new theme, select Text-
Mate → Preferences (⌘ ,), and click the Fonts & Colors tab. The name
of your current theme appears in the pop-up menu at the top of that
panel, and you can switch to a new theme just by selecting a different
name with that menu.

Using this panel, you can also create your own themes from scratch.
This allows you to customize the visual rendering of your documents.
To create a new theme, choose Edit Theme List from the theme name menu
to display the sheet shown in Figure 11.1. You can add a new theme
using the + button in the lower-left corner of this sheet, but it's often
much easier to choose a well-defined theme such as Twilight, click the
++ button to copy the theme, and edit to taste. Either way, you should
immediately type a name for your new theme.

When you are done editing the theme list, dismiss the sheet by clicking
the Okay button; you can then begin editing your new theme. Editing
themes works much like creating preferences. At the top of the theme
panel, you can set default colors for six elements of the document: Foreground, Background, Selection, Invisibles, Line Highlight, and Caret.
In the table below that, you can add elements that optionally override
the Foreground (FG) and Background (BG) colors for specific scopes.

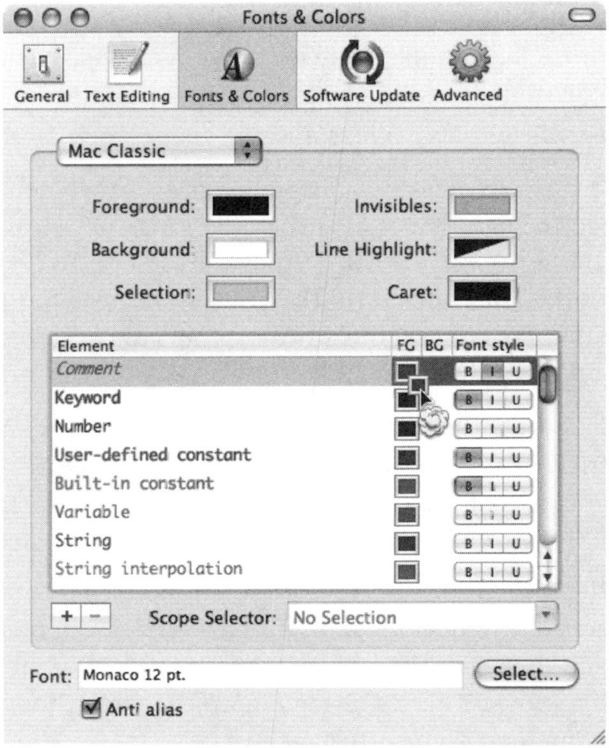

Figure 11.2: REMOVING A COLOR

Elements may also be any combination of bold (B), italic (I), and underlined (U).

To create a new element, follow these steps:

1. Click the + button just below the element list.
2. Type a name for the element. Names should generally be the piece of syntax targeted. You should include the document type if this is not a catchall rule.
3. Click the FG or BG color wells if you want to set either shade. You will be presented with the standard Mac OS X color dialog box from which you can make a choice. TextMate will honor the opacity slider, should you choose to adjust it.
4. Click any combination of the B, I, and U buttons to turn on those style changes. A blue button is active, while clear is off. Just click the button again to toggle its state if you make a mistake.

5. Enter a scope selector for this style, just as you would for an automation or preference file. Only the assigned scopes will be affected. Remember that a more specific scope such as string.quoted.double is always selected over a less specific scope such as string.quoted.

If you make a mistake, you can always remove an element by clicking the name once to highlight it and then clicking the - button beneath the element table. If you want to remove an FG or BG color you set, click and drag the color chit until the cursor changes to display a puff of smoke, and then release the button. You can see this process in Figure 11.2, on the previous page.

If you want to share a theme you created or locate new themes to try on your documents, visit the UserSubmittedThemes page of the TextMate wiki at http://macromates.com/wiki/Themes/UserSubmittedThemes. Double-clicking any .tmTheme file you have downloaded will install it in Text-Mate and make it the active theme.

With this knowledge of how to change TextMate's special behaviors and outward appearance, you have come to the end of what I can teach you in this little book. There's always more to learn, though, so before I close, I'll recommend some other resources.

Chapter 12

Beyond This Book

The hardest part of learning new skills is getting familiar with the jargon associated with them. Congratulations, you're now past that for TextMate. Now that you speak the language, you can talk to others who know the same language. You can start to take advantage of two additional resources available to learn more about the editor. The first is TextMate itself.

Now that you are comfortable with TextMate terminology, try browsing Help → TextMate Help (⌘ ?). The documentation is more for reference and is less example-driven than this text, but you should be ready for that now. The search functionality also makes it valuable for looking up quick answers to questions you may have.

TextMate will continue to evolve after this book is published, and you will be able to get documentation for that too. When you update to a new version, the editor will list the changes. It's a good habit to get into reading these items, because it's the best way to find out about new features. You can access the list for reference anytime you want by selecting Help → Release Notes.

The other sources of knowledge hidden in the editor are the bundles themselves. Some smart individuals have spent a lot of time developing the HTML, Objective-C, Ruby, and Rails bundles, just to name a few. You now know enough to look over these snippets, macros, commands, grammars, and preferences. I promise you'll learn powerful new tricks as you do.

When you get tired of speaking with inanimate objects, it's time to join the TextMate community. We're a lively bunch and are always interested in pushing TextMate to new limits.

Here are the usual hangouts where you can find us:

- The TextMate community keeps up a wiki.[1] The wiki pages have a lot of great resources such as links to cheat sheets; you can find them at http://macromates.com/wiki/Main/UsefulResources.

- You can find instructions for joining the TextMate mailing list at http://lists.macromates.com/mailman/listinfo/textmate.

- Visit the ##textmate[2] IRC channel on Freenode (irc.freenode.net) to speak with TextMate creator Allan Odgaard, me, and the other TextMate regulars.

You can also learn a lot by following Allan Odgaard's TextMate blog at http://macromates.com/blog/ and keeping up with the screencast feed at http://macromates.com/screencasts.

I look forward to seeing you in the community. Be sure to send a hello my way.

---

1. http://macromates.com/wiki
2. Yes, that's two number signs, not a typo. Freenode policy requires the extra character to signify that TextMate is not free software.

Index

Pragmatic Methodology

Welcome to the Pragmatic Community. We hope you've enjoyed this title.

Do you need to get software out the door? Then you want to see how to *Ship It!* with less fuss and more features.

And if you want to improve your approach to programming, take a look at the pragmatic, effective, *Practices of an Agile Developer*.

Ship It!

Page after page of solid advice, all tried and tested in the real world. This book offers a collection of tips that show you what tools a successful team has to use, and how to use them well. You'll get quick, easy-to-follow advice on modern techniques and when they should be applied. **You need this book if:** • You're frustrated at lack of progress on your project. • You want to make yourself and your team more valuable. • You've looked at methodologies such as Extreme Programming (XP) and felt they were too, well, extreme. • You've looked at the Rational Unified Process (RUP) or CMM/I methods and cringed at the learning curve and costs. • **You need to get software out the door without excuses**

Ship It! A Practical Guide to Successful Software Projects
Jared Richardson and Will Gwaltney
(200 pages) ISBN: 0-9745140-4-7. $29.95
http://pragmaticprogrammer.com/titles/prj

Practices of an Agile Developer

Agility is all about using feedback to respond to change. Learn how to apply the principles of agility throughout the software development process • Establish and maintain an agile working environment • Deliver what users really want • Use personal agile techniques for better coding and debugging • Use effective collaborative techniques for better teamwork • Move to an agile approach

Practices of an Agile Developer: Working in the Real World
Venkat Subramaniam and Andy Hunt
(189 pages) ISBN: 0-9745140-8-X. $29.95
http://pragmaticprogrammer.com/titles/pad

Facets of Ruby Series

Curious about the Ruby programming language? Bruce Tate shows you why, when, and how it makes sense to switch *From Java to Ruby*.

Are you a Java programmer interested in learning the Ruby on Rails Web Programming Framework? You don't have to start from scratch: leverage what you already know as you learn *Rails for Java Developers*.

And don't forget our definitive guides to Ruby and to the Rails framework: *Programming Ruby: The Pragmatic Programmer's Guide* and *Agile Web Development with Rails*, now in a new edition.

From Java To Ruby

How can you justify the move away from established platforms such as J2EE? Bruce Tate's *From Java to Ruby* has the answers, and it expresses them in a language that'll help persuade managers and executives who've seen it all. See when and where the switch makes sense, and see how to make it work.

From Java To Ruby: Things Every Manager Should Know
Bruce Tate
(160 pages) ISBN: 0-9766940-9-3. $29.95
http://pragmaticprogrammer.com/titles/fr_j2r

Rails for Java Developers

Enterprise Java developers already have most of the skills needed to create Rails applications. They just need a guide which shows how their Java knowledge maps to the Rails world. That's what this book does. It covers: • The Ruby language • Building MVC Applications • Unit and Functional Testing • Security • Project Automation • Configuration • Web Services This book is the fast track for Java programmers who are learning or evaluating Ruby on Rails.

Rails for Java Developers
Stuart Halloway and Justin Gehtland
(300 pages) ISBN: 0-9776166-9-X. $34.95
http://pragmaticprogrammer.com/titles/fr_r4j

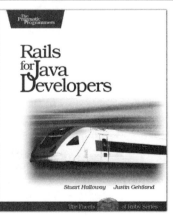

The Pragmatic Bookshelf

The Pragmatic Bookshelf features books written by developers for developers. The titles continue the well-known Pragmatic Programmer style, and continue to garner awards and rave reviews. As development gets more and more difficult, the Pragmatic Programmers will be there with more titles and products to help you stay on top of your game.

Visit Us Online

TextMate
http://pragmaticprogrammer.com/titles/textmate
Source code from this book, errata, and other resources. Come give us feedback, too!

Register for Updates
http://pragmaticprogrammer.com/updates
Be notified when updates and new books become available.

Join the Community
http://pragmaticprogrammer.com/community
Read our weblogs, join our online discussions, participate in our mailing list, interact with our wiki, and benefit from the experience of other Pragmatic Programmers.

New and Noteworthy
http://pragmaticprogrammer.com/news
Check out the latest pragmatic developments in the news.

Save on the PDF

Save PDF version of this book. Owning the paper version of this book entitles you to purchase the PDF version at a terrific discount. The PDF is great for carrying around on your laptop. It's hyperlinked, has color, and is fully searchable.

Buy it now at pragmaticprogrammer.com/coupon.

Contact Us

Phone Orders:	1-800-699-PROG (+1 919 847 3884)
Online Orders:	www.pragmaticprogrammer.com/catalog
Customer Service:	orders@pragmaticprogrammer.com
Non-English Versions:	translations@pragmaticprogrammer.com
Pragmatic Teaching:	academic@pragmaticprogrammer.com
Author Proposals:	proposals@pragmaticprogrammer.com